THE NOBEL BANQUET

PRISMA

Pawel Flato PHOTOGRAPHS

Niklas Lindblad TEXT

TRANSLATED BY Rod Bradbury

The Nobel

Banquet

To my wife Cina and my son Max.
Pawel Flato

P

PRISMA
BOX 2052, TRYCKERIGATAN 4 © 2000 PAWEL FLATO (PHOTOGRAPHS), NIKLAS LINDBLAD (TEXT)
103 12 STOCKHOLM, SWEDEN ROD BRADBURY (ENGLISH TRANSLATION) AND PRISMA, STOCKHOLM
prisma@prismabok.se GRAPHIC DESIGN: CARL ÅKESSON
www.prismabok.se PRINTED IN SWEDEN BY FÄLTH & HÄSSLER, VÄRNAMO 2000
PRISMA PUBLISHERS IS A DIVISION OF P. A. NORSTEDT & SÖNER AB,
FOUNDED IN 1823 ISBN 91-518-3819-2

PREFACE

When I was present at a Nobel Banquet for the very first time, on that occasion as a press photographer, I was completely spellbound by it all. The beautiful light, all the people in their fancy clothes, the sounds and the smells, the magnificent building, the feeling of being at a very special celebration. This is the ball at the palace that Cinderella dreams of attending. The thought of getting away just for a moment from the everyday routine grayness, and warming oneself in the golden lustre. Perhaps the banquet satisfies our need of taking part in a joint ritual, a bigger context. We all take part in the banquet through TV and newspapers and in that way share the experience with the guests. As viewers, we help in our own way to create the festive atmosphere.

I hope that this book will give you the same feeling of fascination and longing that made me take on the project. We all need to go off in our dreams somewhere, sometime.

Pawel Flato

THE GREAT BANQUET • The banquet I shall never forget, making Cinderella's ball pale by comparison? What does it look like, that really incomparable celebration, the one we might experience once in a lifetime? As so often, the simple answer tends to slip away in the redeeming haze of the multitude. For many of us, warm thoughts may reach out to an especially successful and magnificent birthday party, where everything was simply perfect. The weather was ideal, the mix of guests felt both familiar and exciting, and the conversation could range freely between shared experiences and new, unexpected insights. The tables looked really fantastic, what imagination and yet such self-evident simplicity. The table linen and the porcelain, a perfect match of colour and design. The glasses patiently waiting to be filled with drink. The flowers, decorations. It was also the occasion when the food sent a thrill of pleasure through your stomach, when the chef's imagination and skill were in perfect harmony, clear as a bell. The tastes and visual impressions can easily be brought to mind, even though it was quite some time ago.

For once, even the speeches were not only endurable; there were just the right number, bright and precise. In a short time, the speaker said what he or she wanted, and the whole was tastefully spiced with quick wit and humour.

The entertainment was a delight in itself. The master of the music had the good sense to have as his guiding-star that traditional potpourrie of confectionery. Some were done up in fancy shiny silver or gilt paper, filled with truffle and exclusive creams, while others were simply packaged and relied on their candid simplicity. And the music that time, was just like the sweets in the bag – everybody could find something to tempt them out onto the dance floor. And once there, more than one couple found they made music together. No unpleasant incidents, and any possible spicy details that happened to surface, these could discreetly be diverted away before they came to public view.

In a word, when it all had to be tidied away afterwards, and the guests had reluctantly left the party, much later than intended, then the obvious comment was that the organizers had passed with full marks! Dream or reality? Indeed, it may seem more like a dream than reality, but it certainly was reality for me, and nothing else.

And that is what this book is all about: how is it done, how is it achieved, that perfect balance with the delicate mix? The place is Stockholm City Hall, the time is always the 10th of December. And the banquet, the one so keenly covered by the media, is the Nobel Banquet itself. Most of us read about this event in the newspapers, hear about it on the radio or watch it on television. We become consumers, not unlike the poor children of bygone days who pressed their noses to the window pane and looked in upon the candles of the party, the guests and the laden tables. But with the special ability television has to give us an overview as well as a close- up, we may indeed not have been invited but we are nevertheless welcome to take part. Is this a dream that has become reality, or reality as a dream? Both elements are ever present in the minds of those people whose work culminates on Nobel Day in Stockholm.

It is then that the visionary meets the realist, the creative artist whose free-flying thoughts sometimes must plunge to earth when faced with the materialistic cost accounting of the economist. Dreams on the drawing board take form, and are pared down by the practical necessities of reality.

The similarities with life in a theatre suddenly become evi-dent. The date has been fixed for the première, and it seems to be comfortably distant. The players are given their rôles, the workshops make their particular sets, ready plans are followed or changed. But that is also where the comparison with the theatre ends. The Nobel Banquet is given but once a year. A unique performance, where most of the participants are playing their parts for the first and only time. A gala evening, when everything must go right.

So, welcome, honoured guest, to follow us behind the scenes and onto the stage at the banquet of banquets.

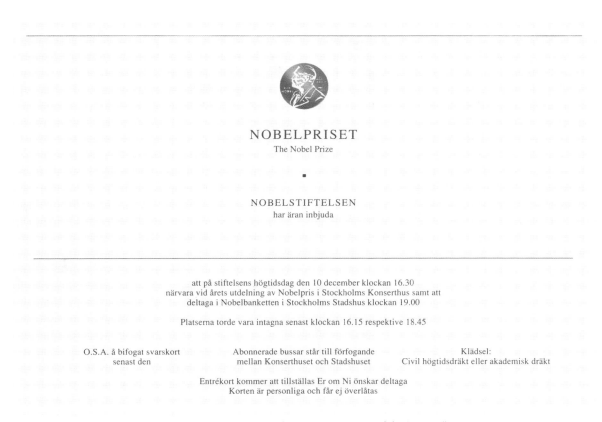

NOBELPRISET
The Nobel Prize

.

NOBELSTIFTELSEN
har äran inbjuda

att på stiftelsens högtidsdag den 10 december klockan 16.30
närvara vid årets utdelning av Nobelpris i Stockholms Konserthus samt att
deltaga i Nobelbanketten i Stockholms Stadshus klockan 19.00

Platserna torde vara intagna senast klockan 16.15 respektive 18.45

O.S.A. å bifogat svarskort Abonnerade bussar står till förfogande Klädsel:
senast den mellan Konserthuset och Stadshuset Civil högtidsdräkt eller akademisk dräkt

Entrékort kommer att tillställas Er om Ni önskar deltaga
Korten är personliga och får ej överlåtas

"The Nobel Prize Committee has the honour to invite ... to the Prize Ceremony and the Banquet"

The Prize ceremony in the Stockholm Concert Hall, on the afternoon of the 10th of December, 1994.

PLANNING AND PREPARATION • The glowing banquet in Stockholm City Hall could be likened to an iceberg, majestically flowing along in polar waters. White and sparkling, it shows only a tenth of its ice mass, while a much greater volume is hidden under the water surface. It is the other nine-tenths that give this colossus its stability and buoyancy, serving as an enormous keel and ensuring that the progress is not prevented by occasional currents or casts of wind.

Or perhaps one ought to compare it with a theatre performance. Or indeed a battle, pure and simple. For months, specialists have planned, predicted, changed and adjusted, all so that the première or battle should follow the lines that have been drawn up. Everything that can reasonably be estimated, assumed, guessed or ascertained, is included in the planning. All that remains, and that can mean surprises, is the actual realization.

But the public are not to know the slightest part of this. Nor do they. In that respect, the comparison with the iceberg is striking: the invisible parts of the calm preparations support the last, brilliant part, which in truth bears scrutiny.

We are now really quite used to how a large part of the world follows what is happening in Stockholm during what is termed Nobel week. Delegations of journalists explain, more or less successfully, the secret behind the discoveries that have led to a particular Nobel Prize. The media reports direct from the homes of the laureates who have to learn a new way of living with their discoveries. Months before the prize ceremony in Stockholm, they are expected to know what the prize money will be spent on, and how their research programmes will develop. And as if that wasn't enough, they often find themselves elevated to the position of some sort of oracle, who is cross-examined in columns and channels as to how one can prevent world starvation, cure all known illnesses and ensure a lasting peace on Earth. For some laureates, undeniably a flying start to life with the Nobel.

It is not only the winner of the Peace Prize who is faced with such questions, although the interest is naturally very great in the Peace Prize laureate(s). Many times, former adversaries have shared this prize, which in the words of Alfred Nobel, in his controversial will, should be awarded to *"the person who has done the most or best work for fraternity between peoples and for the abolition and reduction of standing armies and for the organization and promotion of peace conferences"*. The Peace Prize is presented in Oslo's magnificent City Hall by the Chairman of the Norwegian Nobel Committee in the presence of the Norwegian King and Queen.

The Nobel dinner service must have enough pieces to serve about 1,300 guests – year after year.

For the other laureates in Stockholm, awaits a full and demanding programme with seminars and lectures, embassy visits and cocktail parties, shopping and sight-seeing. Several universities and colleges in Sweden and Norway are visited by the laureates, so there can be quite a lot of travelling during these intensive days. And all the while, the media are trying to gain access to the laureates and their families and supporters, whose comings and goings, and views on everyday issues are seen as being just as interesting as an epoch-making discovery.

But for the public at large, all this is nevertheless the invisible part of the iceberg. For us, the day that counts is the 10th of December itself, Nobel Day, and named as such in the Swedish calender. It is that day which makes Nobel visible and manifest. For the laureates, this is the high spot of their visit in Stockholm, never again will they come to stand in the limelight in quite the same way. The 10th of December is their day.

Grand Hotel – Concert Hall – City Hall. Only a rather small part of our capital city serves as the venue for the foreign guests. Only the most magnificent hotels are good enough for guests who are often seasoned travellers. If you want to book a room in the Grand Hotel in late autumn, then you are going to have difficulties. The last few years, laureates have tended to arrive with increasingly large retinues, and the Grand has not been enlarged to the same extent.

The moment of truth is now approaching, the tail coat is newly pressed, a car has been ordered for the journey to the Concert Hall. The tail coat is not necessarily a problem, but it occasionally can be. Admittedly, the vast majority of the laureates are well versed in the etiquette of academia, and its expectations, but in rare instances this formal dress when worn by one who is uninitiated has been transformed into a terrible instrument of torture with a chafing stiff collar and irritating shirt cuffs.

But having arrived in the festively decorated Concert Hall,

new impressions await, with royal representation, music and, last but not least, the award ceremony. The Grand Auditorium of the Concert Hall is a remarkable venue which copes with the most varied events without ever losing its quintessential quality: a feeling of intimacy. A large, formal event like this one still retains a cosy dimension. And, as so often when nerves are strained, time just vanishes down a black hole. The laureate is suddenly standing there before the King, has received the prize, the diploma and the medal. And, out of earshot of the eavesdropping microphones some personal words to take back home. "And then the King of Sweden said to me…"

Now, the evening could strictly come to an end. With joy complete. Having received such tangible evidence of being one of the chosen, one of the very few.

But, no. There remains an important and time-consuming part of this magnificent day. The dinner, the Nobel Banquet in the Blue Hall of the Stockholm City Hall. The reward, the relaxation, the definite fixing of the triumphal wreath. After all those strained nerves, to at last be able to take one's seat at table, see course after course served, glasses filled, perhaps listen to a speech or two.

How aware are the principal performers of what awaits them at the Nobel Banquet? Certainly, the Nobel Foundation will not even leave this to chance. It pays to reflect a little on this matter. Guests may well have seen television broadcasts on previous occasions, but this dinner will nevertheless exceed their wildest expectations. As a venue for arranging a banquet, the Blue Hall has few rivals that can seat just over 1,200 dinner guests. Immediately, even the simple word 'seat' acquires new content altogether. For each guest a chair, a number of plates, glasses and some cutlery, serviette. If you think of a dinner party in your own home, it is perhaps manageable. Six guests are usually still manageable in most domestic dining rooms. If you have eight guests, then you might not have an even

A few quiet moments. Conductor Michael Bartosch goes through the music a final time before the evening.

In the run-through before the dinner, everything is done to avoid that irritating little word 'perhaps' ever being mentioned by the waiters and waitresses who have the honour of working tonight.

number of everything; with ten or twelve guests then you might have to ask your neighbours for help with chairs, and glasses, which with a little luck will almost match the ones you have already laid out in insufficient number.

But almost 1,300! Help! How should all the guests be seated, so that everyone will enjoy a stimulating and memorable evening? How do you work out how much food and drink will be required? How do you ensure that the food will be kept hot? How will it be possible to serve the right dish at the right time? Where will all the guests' coats be hung, and how can the problem of sufficient lavatories be solved?

PORCELAIN, GLASSWARE AND CUTLERY • On the morning of the 10th of December, in the City Hall designed by Ragnar Östberg. Here, in the Blue Hall – now the large, empty piazza he once envisioned – the morning light is filtered through the windows high up under the ceiling, and the rough brick-walls catch the rays and reflect them on their way. How different the impression would have been of this enormous room, if architect Östberg's early plans to use glass in the roof, had been carried out. The name remains: the Blue Hall.

The stage is yet empty, but the stillness of morning is rudely disturbed as the first actors make their noisy entrance. An unbelievable number of tables and chairs are wheeled in on trolleys. A theatrical display now begins which is highly reminiscent of when an artist works with a few curious observers around him. The canvas is still white, and free of colour, but the artist does not hesitate, his hand fills in the lines and blocks as if they were already sketched in advance. And that is just how the invisible lines on the light marble floor are followed, tables are lined up, gaps checked with measures. It is never a case of 'perhaps'. A fixed number of guests are to be seated. It has been done before but every time is still the first time for those who do the work. The same number of chairs at every

The chef's hat is an essential part of chefs' working clothes.

table, further adjustments and finally the huge equation is solved. The floor is covered with tables which are lined up at a right angle from the long head table, and follow the long sides of the hall. Tables waiting for their linen and porcelain, glasses and cutlery.

Until 1990, the City Hall's own porcelain was used for the Nobel Banquet. A classically strict design with restrained subtlety of nuance, and glasses of a type found in many better restaurants. The following year, the Nobel Prize celebrated its 90th anniversary, and this was clearly reflected in the scale of the arrangements. The Nobel Foundation sent invitations to 140 former laureates, who, with the occasional exception, accepted. Now the Concert Hall would no longer suffice, so the prize-awarding ceremony was moved to the Stockholm Globe and was provided with an imposing framework designed by the head of the Royal Dramatic Theatre, Lars Löfgren. It was in the light of the 90th anniversary that the Nobel Foundation after careful consideration decided to commission a completely new service, including porcelain, glasses, cutlery and table linen. The last time such an order had been placed was in the 1930s, when Sweden's embassies abroad needed to renew their porcelain for entertaining.

So what was so very special about ordering new tableware? It is of course always exciting to have something new. But it was not quite as simple as that. Swedish research and science is richly represented through the various national academies, but with the plans to produce a new service, there arose a desire to give Swedish arts and handicrafts their share of the limelight. The combination of artistry and skill has a good reputation out

Gastronomical briefing. The senior chef at the City Hall Restaurant, Stefan Johnsson (on the right) instructs Per Lindgren, Fredrik Eriksson, Gardar Gislason, Christer Lingström, Gert Klötzke, Torsten Kjörling and Per Ekberg, among others.

The venue of the annual Nobel Banquet – Stockholm City Hall.

Large-scale catering and gastronomic precision at the highest level.

in the world, and visitors to Sweden particularly appreciate Swedish glass.

All the more remarkable that the Nobel Foundation had satisfied itself with borrowed plumes from the City Hall, when on this one occasion every year it was always the focus of world attention. A man who saw potential at an early stage, was Åke Livstedt, art historian. He had previously been noticed when he designed the setting for the Royal Banquet for the 450th jubilee of Gripsholm Palace. He contacted the then managing director of the Nobel Foundation, Stig Ramel, and with his usual enthusiasm compared the Nobel Banquet with a nostalgic trip to a small country town hotel in the 1950s. The comparison was well meant, a dinner in a country town hotel in those days was a high class event as regards the food, the way the table was laid, the linen. What was lacking, according to Livstedt, was that the Nobel Foundation did not present anything of its own that it could exhibit. Here was surely a golden opportunity to market Swedish handicrafts. Unfortunately, this insight happened to coincide with the 1980s financial crisis with the public mood at its most sombre, public initiative at an all-time low. Industry shied clear away, and parts of the Nobel Foundation had little interest in investing in anything new. Spending money on a new service might well be regarded as rashness with the prize money in these dark financial days.

A ceramist at Gustavsberg's Porcelain Factory, Karin Björquist, had designed an everyday service which had been named 'Stockholm', but it had never been put into production. At this time, Gustavsberg was about to be taken over by a Finnish company, and it became all the more clear that the old Swedish idea of beautiful everyday porcelain was no longer economically viable. The idea of re-launching the 'Stockholm' service as a Nobel service, was mothballed, and it was decided to concentrate upon exclusive production for export. Or perhaps they ought really to make an entirely new service, thought

Everywhere behind the scenes, people are preparing for the evening.

Björquist. So it came about that Mr Livstedt, together with architect Magnus Silfverhielm, was given less than two months to formulate his ideas for entirely new tableware. The designer of the new glasses, Gunnar Cyrén, also put forward the idea for the cutlery. Without having any guarantee of buyers, he placed an order with a little, highly specialized Japanese family firm.

On June 6, only six months before the annual celebration, the Nobel Foundation gave its approval. And one ought to bear in mind that it normally takes four years to develop a new porcelain service, and that every part could mean an outlay of up to one million crowns in model and design costs.

The idea behind the Nobel dinner service was to create something that was modern but which still remained within the conventional western concept of tableware for a meal. To cover all that was necessary, with as few pieces as possible, and still combine the aesthetically attractive with the practically functional. The design runs through all the pieces of the service, but also has some unexpected variation, such as the strong border colours of the plates with their symbolic meaning. Green stands for spring, and for the first Nobel Prize in Physics. The colour of summer is a warm white, and the prize is for Chemistry, while autumn glows in a rich orange for the prize in Medicine. Finally, the colour of winter and the prize in Literature, is a deep blue.

There are variations all the time in Karin Björquist's idiom. Her strong warm-white bone china, in one moment sends forth a greeting from the Baroque in a roundly formed bowl or tankard. In the next moment, the guest meets with the strict simplicity of the Japanese table with its mixture of different forms. The beauty lies in the simplicity, as the saying goes. And anyone who has held in their hands, and thought about the form of, a beautiful object, can also imagine the anguish behind these bare essentials. For Karin Björquist and her colleagues at the Gustavsberg factory, the challenges presented themselves one after another, when the many pieces in the service were being formed and fired. In the final table setting, you will find just a little up to the left from the edged plate, a little oddly-shaped bowl with a low edge. It is in actual fact called a "wing" and is common on the continent; in France and Germany it is an essential item. It was used for various 'accessories', such as bread and salad. A playful detail, that for everyday purposes could be used for forming varied presentations. Perhaps a soup bowl in the middle, and four wings around it, a 'déjeuner' with a dip-sauce in the bowl and raw vegetables on the wings.

In summer 1991, Channel 1 of Swedish TV produced a programme entitled 'The Commission'. Among the places we visited was Gustavsberg where we could follow how a lump of clay developed into a decorated piece of porcelain. It was a fascinating experience to see every stage of the process, where the result depended on how successful the preceding process had been. Particularly impressive was our visit to the gold leafers who applied their 24 carat gold to the edges of the plates with thin, flat brushes. I had almost come to the end of my interview with Karin when she started to reach out with her hand behind her back. In a split second, she deliberately flipped up a plate that had been lying just over the edge of the table. The plate flew up in the air, rotated a couple of times and then slammed down onto the floor like a wounded seagull. Karin waited with ill-concealed pride for the plate to come to rest a little way down the room, and then coolly remarked: "I think we have succeeded rather well with the quality this time!" The plate was of course still in perfect condition, and the trick made its intended impression on the innocent film team.

It might seem strange in this context that it was decided to manufacture the cutlery in stainless steel instead of silver, but silver has a greater density than steel, and such solid cutlery

The Blue Hall as a stage. The shiny worn marble is a new experience for the evening's young dancers.

would feel unnecessarily clumsy and heavy in one's hand. The solution was to silver-plate and gild them afterwards, and in this design there is a link to the table silver from King Karl XIV Johan's day, and that silver is still in fact in use in the royal household today. The cutlery is the only part of the order that was not made in Sweden. The quality criteria were simply too high and a little Japanese family firm got the job. One is readily reminded of the smiths who hammered the razor sharp swords of the feudal Samurai.

Gunnar Cyrén, who has been a glass designer at Orrefors glassworks since 1959, paid homage in his series to another great glass designer, Simon Gate, by giving the stems of the glasses strong colours which contrast with all the gilding. Up to the end of the 18th century, the drinking vessel's rôle was very simple and clear. You had but a single goblet or glass. When you wanted your glass filled, you nodded to the wine-waiter, and he rinsed out your glass if necessary and poured in afresh. At that time it became fashionable to serve several, different wines to a meal, and we were blessed with a whole flora of glasses for different purposes.

The Nobel glasses are just as many as are needed so that all the drinks we associate with a large banquet can be served elegantly and suitably. Particularly chameleon-like is the champagne glass, which can also be filled both with hors d'œuvres and sweets. You could call it a sort of all-round glass and it would do very well on an everyday dinner table too, if you fill it with low-alcohol beer or mineral water.

TABLE LINEN • When we bring out our finest family linen tablecloth for a dinner party at home, our thoughts tend to go out to the person from whom we inherited it. Taking out the heavy cloths and then moistening and putting them through the mangle, is all a part of the preparations for a successful dinner. The Nobel tablecloths and serviettes were woven by the Klässbol Linen Weavers in Värmland. Ingrid Dessau, when she designed them, used a modern idiom with the traditional technique. Here, too, it was a case of balancing between making the cloths an inherent part of the table service and showing something quite different. The porcelain is of course warm and white in colour, and the cloth's coarse, silver-grey linen yarn provides a necessary contrast, which lets all the parts of the whole have their say. The tablecloths are woven in a diaper pattern, a primitive damask with a large diamond check which reflects the light differently from the warp and the weft surfaces. The cloth changes in shade and appears different, depending on from which side you look at it, and where the light is coming from.

And this, of course, particularly pleased the television lighting technicians and cameramen, who have always battled with the white table cloths, trying to make them seem a little less harsh on screen. For them, the matt silver surface of the linen and the chequered pattern, were like a gift from above. At last, the surfaces of the large tables became a possible subject for the camera, placed up high and looking down onto the banquet with a bird's eye view. Those abhorrent dazzling reflections were a thing of the past, and although the cloths were now in fact silver-grey, the colour nuances are transformed by the cameras and the receivers to the desired shade that we see as white.

It is amusing to reflect upon the fact that in olden days a serviette was purely used to protect your clothes. The hygienic detail of wiping your mouth with it, came later. Originally bread was used for that purpose, and as a greeting from former times, bread is now sometimes placed inside a simply folded serviette. For this, Ingrid Dessau chose a semi-bleached linen yarn woven in damask. The diamond pattern is repeated round the medal with Alfred Nobel's portrait, which appears in relief.

THE WAITERS AND WAITRESSES • So, these are now the various pieces that will go to deck out all those tables on the 10th of December. The measures that will regulate how and where the tables shall be placed are both impartial and ruthless, the number of guests is once and for all limited to about 1,300. The hall must not feel crowded, even if it is. Everything is measured out, including the distance between the tables, the chairs, the plates, the glasses. Perhaps not unlike the way generals draw up their armies for the impending battle. Working clothes for today include thin, white gloves – there are to be no finger prints on the glasses or the cutlery. There is a lot going on, a whole range of different professionals are involved, each with some specialist knowledge. Serving at the dinner are an incredible 210 waiters and waitresses.

Many of the serving staff regard the evening as so special, that they come back year after year. Almost an honorary position, one could say, an occasion to proudly display their skills before an enormous public. But the City Hall Restaurant thinks it wrong to always use exactly the same staff, so each year about thirty new hopefuls are tested for the event.

THE CHEFS AND THE MENU • The path to today's televised banquet in the Blue Hall has of course been long and varied. The dinner after the first prize-awarding ceremony in 1901 was held in the Hall of Mirrors at the Grand Hotel. By today's standards, it was a rather modest affair with a hundred or so guests, and it was a subscription dinner. The menu, however, was not at all modest, and consisted of 7 to 8 courses. It was a mammoth dinner of a bygone sort, which might include a clear consommé, a fish course, a meat course, bird, a salad dish, and something sweet followed by pastries. One would imagine that the dance afterwards would have been a welcome feature, if the ladies wanted to dance at all. Because they were only welcome once the actual dinner was over.

The food rationing which resulted from the First World War, meant that some of the excesses were reduced, and from 1919 the dinner was cut down to a manageable four courses: soup, fish, meat and sweet. The venue of the dinner was moved in the 1920s to the newly built City Hall, where the mosaic in the Golden Hall framed the festive meal. In 1945, the menu was altered again, and now they were down to three courses. Popular fish such as sole and turbot pleased the guests, as did snow grouse. It was what we used to call 'exclusive food' at restaurants. An orthodox, safe and not particularly exciting fare many would say today, now that we are accustomed to variety, new ingredients and the joy of experimentation in the kitchen.

In the kitchens of the City Hall, there is one saying that is most definitely out of place. "Too many cooks spoil the broth" is of course totally ridiculous. This day and evening requires more chefs than any other occasion. Between 25 and 30 are needed, and there is no difficulty in finding candidates. As with the waiters and waitresses, there are many who like to come back year after year, and some are hopeful newcomers who have been carefully selected to show what they can do together with experienced old hands. Many feel called, but only few are chosen – the profession is becoming all the more popular. The Swedish Chef of the Year members have provided inspiration since the mid-Eighties. Members can take part five times at most, then others take over to ensure continuity.

A major problem when you invite guests to a large dinner party is that you do not always remember which of the guests have previously had the good fortune to taste your particular speciality. You do not want your guests to think that you only master one dish! In the City Hall Restaurant, they do not take the risk. Restaurateur Lars-Göran Andersson and his team of chefs are faced with a rather different problem than ordinary party arrangers who book a special venue for one single

The calm before the storm. For the guests in the Blue Hall, the cooks are a group of specialists who are active in the background.

celebration dinner. It is easier to 'go all out', and concentrate one's resources for the occasion, and the choice of food is in many ways more focused. In the case of the City Hall Restaurant, they always have a tight schedule and the various menus must replace each other at express speed. It is admittedly pleasant to be fully-booked, but it demands a completely different approach to planning.

Early in the spring, the chefs start airing their ideas. What is feasible, what has the menu looked like the past four, five years, how often can a dish be repeated? Perhaps one could make a variation of a particularly successful and appreciated dish from before? When they have agreed upon several interesting suggestions, perhaps four menus, then these are sent to the Nobel Foundation. As befits it, the Foundation always seems to include several members who are interested in wine and food, and these provisional menus are subject to a critical examination already at this stage. The organizers still have an open mind, because as yet they have no idea as to the nationality of the laureates, or which religion they represent. Nor do they yet know what general theme the Blue Hall will have that evening – heat, cold, winter or whatever. In late September, the Foundation samples the various menus, finely-attuned palates evaluate, and the winning menu is decided upon so that the City Hall Restaurant can go ahead with its planning. After this, little is changed as regards spices or other details. It is necessary to know with certainty that the chosen menu can be followed through, that all the fresh produce and other ingredients really will be available. At the 1990 banquet, the menu included char from Lake Vättern, a delicacy that could only be served up thanks to useful contacts with the lake's professional fisherman who 'reserved' the considerable quantity of fish required.

Early in the 1900s it must have been a formidable challenge to be responsible for such a large dinner. There were no deep freezes for storage, hardly any greenhouse vegetables to vary the menu with. But even if today's chefs have a lot more room for manoeuvre than their former colleagues, they still have to bear in mind what lies within the framework of possibility. The Nobel Prize celebrated its 90th jubilee in 1991, and the determined efforts to further heighten the splendour around the ceremony and the banquet were of course reflected in the menu.

The think-tank behind the dinner's processions and entertainment had chosen the number '4' as their central theme. The brand new Nobel dinner service was to be inaugurated, and the plates with their edges in four colours represented the four seasons of the year. Spring came first, and the first course was to be soup. And what could possibly be more springlike, they reflected, and yet still exotically Swedish, than nettle soup? But nettles in December? Again, the answer lay in having useful contacts with the suppliers. Thanks to early planning, the Findus company in Skåne could pick enough nettles, and these were then par-boiled before being frozen, labelled 'City Hall Restaurant'. Amazed, and presumably envious colleagues, are said to have asked how on Earth they had managed to do it! The City Hall restaurateur only had one regret – he had not been able to crown his soup with a fresh, crisp nettle leaf.

Sometimes what might seem a fairly common or garden product, can turn out to be rather awkward to get hold of. For the dinner in 1989, it had been decided to have elk fillet steak as the hot dish. It ought to be easy enough to get hold of in Sweden where a large numbers of elk are shot during the autumn hunting season every year. But it soon transpired that elk fillet was not a common item with the wholesalers, because most of the meat ended up in the hunters' own freezers. But that time too, it was possible to serve the promised elk fillet as though it was the most natural thing in the world.

The Nobel Banquet is broadcast on Swedish television and is also covered by many members of the international press.

The Master of Ceremonies, Jan Hartman (on the right) carries the heavy ceremonial staff, a gift from the Nobel Foundation to the City Hall in gratitude for all the good cooperation over the years.

But it is not just the potential difficulties in acquiring the desired ingredients that can cause problems. Sometimes a visionary chef has very special requirements as to how his particular dish should be prepared and served. His or her thoughts must then be realized in the best way possible. In an ordinary restaurant kitchen it would certainly be possible to do so for a normal number of guests, but when it comes to the banquet on the 10th of December in the Blue Hall, there are no 'normal' proportions. On one occasion, for example, it had been decided to serve an exciting hors d'oeuvre consisting of an artichoke resting on a slice of dark bread garnished with some lobster and a cream made from salmon. No problems with the ingredients this time, the delicious salmon was smoked in Laholm and everyone who had sampled the dish had been delighted. The dish was to be named 'Artichoke timbale' and its form was thus obvious. So far, so good. But where could they find 1,300 timbale moulds? To have new ones made, would have been prohibitively expensive. The restaurateur, who was trying to think of solutions even when he was at home, happened to need something for his house so he visited a builders' merchants. Among all the items he caught sight of a long plastic pipe with a diameter just the same as the one for the timbale form. He purchased a little bit of piping, and had it sawn up into small pieces. He then lined the pipe stumps with cling film, prepared the dish and baked it in the oven. It worked perfectly, and the builders' merchants soon received a large order for plastic pipes and were also informed that the customer was not a building company, but a restaurant which was going to 'build' food in the forms.

Being able to work in a kitchen that is well-designed and practical, often means you are already half way there to a successful result. When the City Hall architect, Ragnar Östberg, planned the building, any thought of practical kitchens must however have been very distant. The kitchen areas are at the

The guests arrive by limousine as well as on foot.

very top of the building, and the serving staff have to go up and down lots of winding staircases during the evening. Detailed planning is required for staff logistics if the various time schedules are to be adhered to. Somebody is said to have estimated that each waiter and waitress walks more than five kilometres during the Nobel Banquet evening.

How long the dinner has actually gone on for, has varied over the years and still varies. In the 1970s and 1980s, the guests sat at table for about three hours, while the 1990s has seen dinners lasting almost four hours. As with all dinners, the eating itself only accounts for a smaller part of the time – it is the company and the conversations that makes the time seem to fly. Sometimes, the well-placed guests lose themselves in joint interests, and simply forget to eat their food. It can be a rude awakening when the still half-laden plate is whisked away from the table and disappears off with the waiter. Naturally, this is not done maliciously, but the evening is planned in detail and the plans must be followed. The restaurateur keeps an eye on the situation, and when about 95% of the guests have finished a course, then he gives the sign to his troops. Not even a gallantly conversing former Minister of Finance succeeded in keeping his plate, when the wave of waiters swept forth at the appointed moment.

But the guests certainly do not have to gobble their food down, by no means, for long experience and the use of stopwatches means that the organizers know just how much time is needed for most dishes and courses. The actual eating rarely takes more than 14 or 15 minutes per course, with a little leeway, depending on how complicated the food is, that is being served. Perhaps the hors d'œuvres only takes 12 minutes, and then a little extra time can be allowed for the hot dish, or vice versa.

"But isn't that...?" The 1999 Literature laureate, Günter Grass arrives in style in a limousine.

THE SERVICE • And yes, I did say 'hot dish'. And there is of course a problem here. How can they serve 1,300 guests with hot food which has to be carried down from a kitchen which is quite some distance away? An immediate response might be that the food must be prepared in advance, and then kept hot in some effective manner. But food that is kept in a warming oven for some time, will rarely contribute to the efforts of an ambitious chef. Let us take the hot dish in 1999 as a brilliant and informative example. They served a delicate outer fillet of lamb wrapped in cabbage. The meat had been quickly browned on the outside in advance, and was still raw, the cabbage had only been lightly parboiled. The dish was then formed with its trimmings, these also being prepared ready for the oven, and then placed on special trolleys in a cold store, waiting to be wheeled along to the Golden Hall early in the evening to the waiting circo-therm ovens. This dish was prepared in a test run so that they knew that the meat would acquire its fine, pink colour after 18 minutes in the oven, neither more nor less. And the exact starting time was worked out by simply counting backwards. It takes 5 minutes to serve the wine, 4 to hand out the plates for the hot dish, and 4 to place the sauce and potatoes on the tables. Add the time necessary to get everything there and back, and you come to 18 minutes. The chefs should therefore start their ovens, set at 80 degrees the very moment the first course is cleared away. Considering the above, it is understandable that any guest who has not finished eating, Minister of Finance or not, will see his or her plate taken out together with all the others. Anything else would be like trying to stop a supertanker because a member of the crew dropped his mobile phone in the sea.

Having got so far, we know that the food is hot and how it has become hot, but the question remains: How can it be kept hot all the way to the tables?

When the procession of waiters and waitresses winds its way down the broad staircase which leads from the Golden Hall to the Blue Hall, the old, classic serving salvers can be seen to have been replaced with oven-proof ceramic ware. Silver salvers are of course a much grander way of presenting food, but they have a drawback in that they lose heat so quickly. Ceramic ovenware with a high rim, can keep its contents hot for much longer.

It is also possible to choose dishes that are known to retain their temperature a long time. The Nobel menu the last few years has included creamed potatoes in various forms. It can be transported without cooling down, and can be varied endlessly, for example with some Cheddar cheese and pieces of the underrated delicacy, black salsify. This is the same sort of challenge that a musical composer is faced with, when he has a really good and catchy theme in his head. That theme then comes to form the stable basis for his continued work: variations are permitted to veer off in different directions. Some will be easily recognizable, being close in style, while others will have gone off on winding, dizzying journeys. If you hear the words 'creamed potatoes', it might not sound particularly exciting, but in the hands of a creative chef, and in classic menu-French there is a transformation: "Purée fine de pommes de terre au cheddar". And this can be varied ad infinitum.

As in all fields, fashion influences the art of preparing food. It can mean the difference between success and failure for a restaurant, if it can catch an emerging trend at the right moment, and then judge how long it is going to last. In the context of the Nobel dinner, the influence of fashion is restricted by virtue of the very special circumstances, such as the distance between the kitchens and the guests, and the problem of keeping food hot as described above.

So the rather long-lived trend of building up very high, visually effective dishes, passed without trace in the City Hall kitchens. Some people thought that this was a pity, as half the

With the right sort of lighting, the ceiling of the Blue Hall 'opens up' and it seems as if it hovers above the rough brick walls.

pleasure of food lies in the eye of the beholder. Beautiful creations which tower above the platter, linked by delicate ribbons of finely chopped vegetables. Regrettably, towers of food are not suited to the walk of several minutes that the waiters have to undertake, and most particularly the final stretch down the magnificent staircase of rather worn Kolmården marble which connects the Golden Hall with the Blue Hall. Despite a number of test walks with empty platters down these steps, many of the selected waiters have felt the butterflies move down in their stomachs when the evening arrives, and it is the real thing.

But these butterfly carriers are in good company. When architect Ragnar Östberg had decided where the stairway was to be sited, he took no risks. He built up a full-scale wooden model, and experimented with treads and risers of varying size, well aware that this was not just an ordinary stairway. He created a stairway for processions. A stairway that was to be part of a show. The final trials were carried out by the architect's wife, in a full evening dress, who was to ascertain the most suitable dimensions for the steps. The architect had a clear vision when creating his stairway: one should be able to admire the guests as they descended the stairs, without worrying that someone might trip up. He made the treads somewhat deeper, and the risers somewhat lower than is normal, which accounts for the special, elegantly flowing pace. The first time, you are not really aware why it feels different, the steps seem to meet your feet before you expect it. Not until you have walked up and down the stairway a couple of times, does it feel comfortable.

So, even if all the serving staff are well acclimatized to the stairway, the chefs do not take the risk of towering displays of food. They also avoid 'cross-over' in which there is an uninhibited mixing of elements from the cuisine of different continents. But a successful restaurateur does not establish his realm by avoiding things, he has to somehow tread that tightrope, even though he might find it hard to retain his balance along the way. The customers who sit at his tables on December 10, do not form a homogeneous group of restaurant guests. With so many different nationalities, religions and ages, anything extreme when it comes to the food, must be ruled out. One could perhaps summarize the ambitions by saying that they 'try to renew in a sustainable manner'. From traditional starting points, exciting novelties and details can be served up, taking what works well from different trends. In recent years, the choice of food also reflects a desire to serve ingredients from Sweden's own forests and waters. 'Fancy food' might go down well, but it is likely that guests from both far and near will already be acquainted with fillet steak and Dover sole in some form or other. A special element in the banquet in the City Hall, is that it should give the guests a culinary experience which they will come to remember, dishes where the ingredients were so tasty that the sensation will remain etched into one's palate for a long time to come. Reindeer fillet, char mousse, sauces with wild mushrooms and berries from the Swedish forests…

It is late afternoon on the 10th of December. It has already been dark for several hours. The enormous floor of the Blue Hall is covered with perfectly straight rows of tables, lined up at a right angle from the head table. There is a faint glow from the newly polished glasses and cutlery, and the white china seems to hover above the silver-coloured tablecloths. As yet, the air above Ragnar Östberg's piazza is light and clear, and the sounds of the last preparations can be heard from somewhere distant. The set design and the props are all ready and in place. The curtain can soon once again rise on the Blue Hall's annual and only première and performance: the Nobel Banquet.

EVENING DRESS • When we set out on a journey to a distant country with another climate, we have to use our imagination as regards what clothes to pack, so we do not find

The 'evening of the limousines' in the courtyard of the City Hall.

ourselves short of something important when we arrive. Is it going to be warmer or colder than at home? Rain or sunshine? The travel brochures have pictures of the ideal weather conditions, or of how they would like it to be, and are thus rarely of any real help. So how do the laureates and their families picture our weather, in this long stretched-out country which reaches beyond the Arctic Circle? The myth of polar bears roaming the streets of Stockholm in a bitingly cold arctic climate, is hopefully losing credibility, and perhaps the problem is really of no consequence. Most of what is planned for these guests from far-off lands, is by necessity intended to take place indoors, in which instances 'informal dress' is quite adequate. It can be amusing sometimes to catch a glimpse of what a research scientist – with his mind focussed on other things – regards as elegant in this context. Loose-fitting, warm tweed jackets seem to be a popular garment. But all the laureates have at least been informed about the correct choice of indoor clothing for the banquet evening. For ladies it is an evening gown, and for gentlemen, a tailcoat.

There would be no problem at all, if we had a dinner where all the guests came from the armed services. The order of the day would be full dress uniform, and while this may vary in style and cut, a uniformed guest would be confident of being formally and properly attired regardless of where he came from. But this is not the case with regard to the tailcoat. Some guests will not have come into contact with this garment other than when it has been worn by a head waiter at a restaurant. With a little luck, a tailcoat can be hired in the laureate's home country, but if that country lacks a 'tailcoat tradition', then male guests must make sure they can order a garment in good time. The firms in Stockholm that rent out formal dress have a particularly busy time around the 10th of December; acute

shortages can be expected. On several occasions, I have found myself next to a fitting room where future laureates have struggled with the unusual details of their rented attire, and their questions have sometimes been amusing to eavesdrop on. But sometimes it does not seem to matter however well prepared you are, and how often you have checked that everything is in place. One year, just before we were to go on air with the television broadcast, one of my colleagues discovered that the breast pocket opening of my tailcoat was ominously black and empty. Shock and panic! As luck would have it, we had earlier that evening eaten dinner at the City Hall Restaurant and I had, for some reason, pocketed an extra serviette 'which might come in handy during the evening'. It was admittedly made of paper, but when rapidly folded with three symmetrical points protruding, it appeared on television to be a well ironed formal handkerchief, as good as any that come!

THE GUESTS ARRIVE • Picture postcard weather, or not, the guest who arrives via the gateway on the north side, from Hantverkargatan, can hardly refrain from stopping for a moment, just to take in the scene before him. A few steps will take the guest through the archway and into the courtyard, from where the City Hall can be seen in all its majesty. The courtyard is enclosed on all sides; towards the left, is the massive bell-tower with its three golden crowns 106 metres up above. To the right, the lights from the Golden Hall glow through the five, high arched windows, warm and welcoming. But what is most striking on this first visit, must surely be the view straight ahead, towards the south. Architect Östberg has succeeded admirably in picking up that worn-out phrase about Stockholm being the Venice of Scandinavia, and putting it into practice. The southern façade opens up in a series of arches, resting on massive pillars in double rows, so that the observer has a free view out over Riddarfjärden bay, across to the

heights of Södermalm. An evening like this, the large outdoor candles are packed all along the balustrade down to the water, and the effect is like an illusion of a well-crafted perspective painting, whether the candle flames are reflected in ice or open water.

How might guests be expected to react to this marvellous view? For some of the regular guests, this evening is another dinner in familiar surroundings, and they quickly make their way in through the tower entrance across to the right. Most guests, however, when they come upon this view, tend to stop for a few moments, perhaps make some comments. But, if truth be told, it is not just the view that delays them, for here, beside the stairs leading to the cloakrooms, are large hordes of photographers. And the surprisingly tempting, concentrated light from the television spotlights.

QUEUES • It is fascinating to note the various tactics that come into play, when a celebrity just 'happens' to enter the camera's field of vision. At first, he or she seems to be looking in all directions, until this seems untenable and then the publicity-hungry celebrity looks unabashedly straight into the camera. It has not always been so easy for me as a reporter to interview the guests I wanted to, and I have often had to accept the motto of the pop artist Andy Warhol that every person has the right to be famous for fifteen minutes of his life.

The first traffic jam of the evening, is at the cloakroom. The City Hall has well-dimensioned facilities, but when 1,300 guests deposit their outer garments in a short time, then it is essential that the cloakroom attendants know what they are doing. The choice of dress for the evening means that both the ladies' and gentlemen's outer garments all look very much alike. Fur coats and topcoats tend to be in the same style, so if you mislay your number it will be a nightmare to retrieve your coat later in the evening.

And some guests have to retrieve their coats sooner than expected. A pair of spectacles, that essential little book with the seating plan, where did they get to?

The next stop en route, is the lavatory, and here even a very modest number of guests can lead to overrunning the tight schedule in an alarming manner. An episode from 1991, when the Nobel Prize had its 90th jubilee, deserves to be related. The Nobel Foundation had invited all surviving laureates and the Concert Hall was discovered to be far too small for the prize-awarding ceremony, so it was decided to move the occasion to the newly-opened Stockholm Globe. The banquet, however, would still be held in the City Hall according to plan, and this was an equation that required a special solution. All the transport logistics had been carefully prepared, many buses had been booked for the occasion and the underground railway ran special 'Nobel trains', coloured blue, of course! So far, so good, the only stumbling block was the lavatories. The guests would probably – or so reasoned the planners – quickly leave the Globe and hasten to the waiting buses to make sure they would arrive at the City Hall and its lavatories in good time. And these lavatories would not be able to cope. For the gentlemen, the solution was a number of small metal huts known in Sweden as 'Baja-Maja', a typically Swedish term more suited to young children and defying translation (an equivalent British convenience is more successfully termed 'Portaloo'), and these were strategically placed in the City Hall courtyard, and were painted Nobel blue in honour of the great day.

It was more difficult to accommodate the ladies, and when the organizers finally found a solution, this was as simple as it was rather an embarrassment. There was agreement as to the fact that a visit to the Ladies' Room took longer than necessary because there was a mirror for every visitor. Would it be possible to reduce the average length of a visit to the Ladies' Room,

The Nobel Banquet as a gigantic theatre performance with the best dressed actors in the world – in public and behind the scenes.

This is mass catering in style. The serving trolleys in the Golden Hall are overshadowed by Einar Forseth's magnificent mosaics.

by the simple expedient of removing every second mirror? No sooner said, than done. And lo and behold, the throughput increased, the dinner could begin exactly on time, and most remarkable of all – the complaints expected, were never made.

The area around the cloakrooms is a natural gathering place while waiting for the start of the evening's festivities, so that guests may take their seats. There is a tremendous atmosphere, and the noise is tremendous too, it is crowded and it soon gets very warm. An observant guest will find this a most pleasant start to the evening – you can examine your fellow guests and their evening dress. Jewellery is discreetly noted, decorations and medals too. Veterans greet their acquaintances with a nod, while guests who are there for the first time try to notice everybody, acquaintances and strangers alike.

THE SEATING PLAN • Much of what happens during the evening, many of the guests have experienced in previous banquets on a smaller scale. To be able to dress to the nines, and then be full of expectations as to a successful and enrichingly festive dinner. But the very scale of the Nobel dinner makes all other dinners pale in comparison. Take the seating plan, for example; at a normal-size dinner it suffices to discreetly cast an eye over the name cards placed out on the tables. You might not yet know who is who, but some names usually stick in your memory. But that method is not applicable when there are about 1,300 guests. Naturally, there are elegant small name cards beside every setting, but that does not help much when the table of honour is 40 metres in length, and there are 24 long tables fanning out from this, plus a further 20 smaller tables. Any approaching panic can however be stilled by recourse to the elegant little seating book that has been handed out to each and every guest, and which indicates the correct table and place with the help of numbers. There is plenty to read there, but because it also details the title of every guest,

you can usually observe waiting couples deeply engrossed in what the evening may have to offer by way of familiar guests.

With the book to safely guide them, the guests seek out their places and it is now they meet their partners at table for the almost four-hour long banquet. Curiosity and expectation! How will the conversation develop? Will we have some shared interests and if so, in what fields?

The printed programme sheet indicates that guests should be at their seats by 18.45, and that the actual dinner shall start at 19.00. It is a nice thought to give the guests a little time to get to know one another, but the planners have other things in mind too. They want to be certain that all the guests are in their proper places when the trumpet fanfare sounds on the stroke of seven, announcing that the head table's honoured guests, led by the Royal Couple, are now approaching the hall balcony in a procession that runs along one of the long sides of the Golden Hall.

A RATHER SPECIAL EXPERIENCE • I can imagine that everyone would like to be present, at least once in a lifetime, at an event that really overwhelms them. It can be the event itself, or the very scale of it, that would take your breath away, or it could be the people present and those who are sharing the experience. Many people will gladly mention their wedding as just such an event. Your friends and acquaintances gathered together in a light, beautiful place with music under the arched ceiling. A tense expectation, perhaps even nervousness is in the air, and there is no doubt as to who (for once) is at the centre of attention.

Something of the same feeling is present when the clock strikes seven, and the evening begins for the guests in the Blue Hall.

The television lighting technicians push all the switches on their control panels. The Blue Hall is brilliantly lit-up, and

light shines into every last corner of the enormous room, all 1,526 square metres of it. The City Hall organ, the largest in Scandinavia, comes to life, concealed behind its ornamental front just under the ceiling, 22 metres above the marble floor. It can be rather alarming when the organist lets loose with all those 10,271 pipes, their sound divided over 138 stops, playing something suitable for a slow procession in step. The last ten years or so, the trumpeter has added a little variety to the musical accompaniment during the majestic entrance by playing a fanfare, and the procession is now led, as of old, by a Master of Ceremonies with a staff. This is a striking piece, donated in 1991 by the Nobel Foundation to the City Hall as a token of gratitude for their co-operation. The staff is of alder wood, crowned with the City Hall tower in silver, austerely designed by Gunnar Cyrén. It is of considerable weight and it must be quite demanding for the leader of the procession to carry this over the floor of the balcony, worn smooth by the passage of a myriad of feet, and down the magnificent staircase.

This is the guests' first meeting with the King and Queen, the laureates and the other guests of honour. Heads are turned, and necks are stretched to catch a glimpse of the Queen's tiara and dress, high up on the balcony. And over there, the Literature Laureate, who is he taking to table? The procession now veers off to the left down the staircase, and more of the guests down in the Blue Hall are able to see the King with the lady he is escorting to table, who is either a laureate, or, if there is no female laureate, the wife of the eldest Physics Laureate. The Queen is escorted by the Chairman of the Nobel Foundation, and they are followed by the laureates and ambassadors and other guests of honour, couple by couple.

With the intensive television coverage, there is considerable pressure on all those taking part to know exactly what they are expected to do, and when. If something goes wrong and there is a 'traffic jam', the effect is magnified by the cameras,

and even the slightest hesitation is noticed in one way or another. So this first, distinguished procession has also been put through a trial run, albeit in concentrated form. Every couple is instructed as to how they should part, walking along either side of the head table, when they get to the foot of the staircase. Do not even consider the possibility that someone might go down the wrong side, and then realize it was wrong and try to go back and round without being seen. It has never happened yet.

Each guest has been provided with a thin programme which presents the menu in orthodox restaurant French. And several fixed times, of which two will already have passed when the guests and the guests of honour are all seated at table. At 19.05, the Chairman of the Nobel Foundation proposes a toast to the King, and two minutes later the King in turn proposes a toast to Alfred Nobel, "the Great Donator". The next fixed time is 22.00 hours, when the signal is given to rise from the table. The Royal Family then receive the laureates in private, and the dancing begins. Otherwise, everything that happens during the evening is a surprise.

But a quick peep in the programme can perhaps provide inspiration for the first words addressed to the unknown lady or gentleman sitting adjacent at table. Considering that Swedish publishers issued about eighty books on culinary matters in 1998, then both you and your partner might well be interested in such a subject. Or perhaps your partner is knowledgeable enough to comment on the wines that will accompany the food. But this, however, is still a matter for expectation and conjecture – nobody has yet been awarded a Nobel Prize for personal chemistry!

In the case of a formal banquet, it becomes a fine art to place guests so that they all feel the evening has been a success, and that the company has been stimulating. Mr Stig Ramel, the Managing Director of the Nobel Foundation between

The king of Literature in 1999, Günter Grass with a knowledgeable public.
Princess Christina and the Medicine laureate, Günter Blobel listen and learn.

1972 and 1991, considers this aspect of the preparations as particularly demanding but also rewarding. It matters little that the visual impressions, the food, the drink, the well-laid tables and the decorations are first class, if you are unable to communicate with your partner at table. So Mr Ramel's successor, and his trusted colleagues, put a great deal of energy into matching the 1,300 guests as though they were pieces of a giant jigsaw puzzle, that had to fit on all sides. It may seem tempting to let a computer, or some other mechanical device, do the heavy work, but this is not a feasible alternative. It is a case of getting to know something about a thousand people, which sort of table companion would suit them best, someone with whom would they have something in common? The reward, as Stig remembers it, was in the form of guests who afterwards thanked him for the successful placing, and wondered which crystal ball he had gazed into! The present Managing Director, Mr Michael Sohlman, remembers a lady guest who was seated between two foreign professors. This was just spot on; it quickly transpired that all three had shared interests, so shared indeed that the lady and one of the gentlemen are now sharing their lives.

To go by people's interests might seem a rather clumsy method, but it works surprisingly often. It helps a little that the invitation is accompanied by a couple of questions about which languages the recipient speaks and which interests he or she has. One method which is definitely not to be recommended, is to be seated beside your husband or wife. The whole point of the seating plan is that it should provide the possibility to

"Oh! What a dreadfully long party!" Sitting at table for up to four hours is experienced in different ways by different generations.

The Queen with the 1999 Physics Laureate, Martinus Veltman.

discover new things and perhaps establish new and valuable contacts for the future. To insist on a safe card like a family member, will not get you a seat in the limelight during the dinner.

For certain categories of guests, being placed among peers nevertheless works well. Subject specialists feel very comfortable in their home waters, and always seem to have much to discuss with each other.

So what is actually needed, to be graced with the much sought-after invitation to the City Hall? Many hopefuls do not just sit idly waiting, they write or phone the Foundation and ask favours for someone near and dear. A Nobel dinner is seen as a perfect 50th birthday present, and many are the letters that elegantly ask for the chance to give this memory of a lifetime. But unfortunately, however deserving the cause may be, this is not a practicable way to get to the table. Nor the fact that the supplicant is a Swedish citizen, or pays for a television licence. The dinner in the Blue Hall is a private party, held by the Nobel Foundation for guests who have been of service to the Foundation or the prize-awarding scientific institutions, or donated money. Period.

But even so, every year it is uncertain if the puzzle is going to be solved, and all the invited guests fitted in. In September, invitations are sent out to about 2,000 people. Students, our future research scientists, are always included as singing or parading elements and 250 seats are set aside for them. The number of laureates varies from year to year, but their families and the rest of their entourage, will soon fill a further 150 seats. Some guests send word they are unable to attend, and the winter influenza season usually takes its toll, as does the ice on the pavements; so the equation usually works out in the end.

But you have to reply to the invitation in good time. On one occasion, one of the leading figures in Swedish industry phoned to say that a journey abroad, or something similar, had

The Queen's jewellery is the cause of much curiosity.

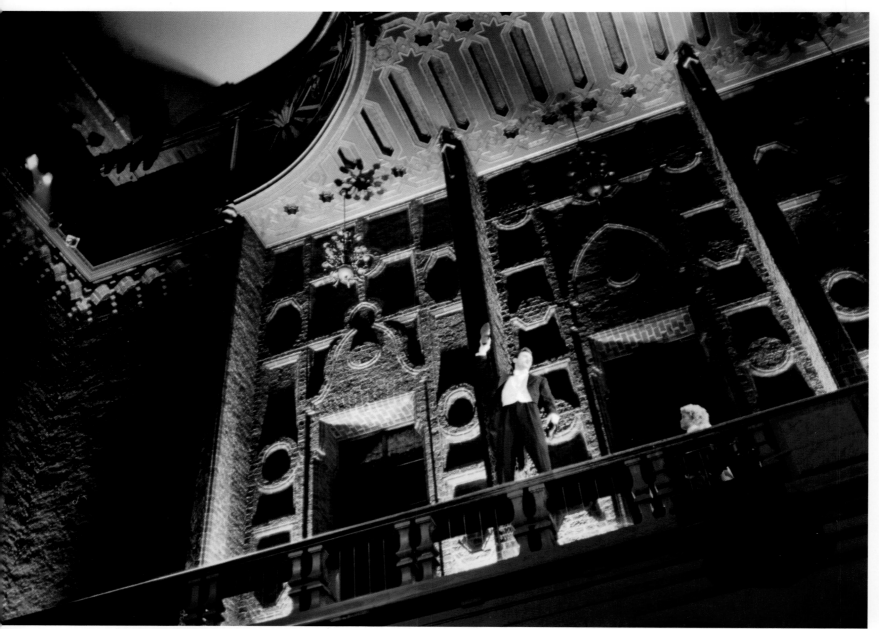

Dinner entertainment on a high level. Striking and risky balancing act on the well-worn balustrade 9 metres above the guests' heads.

meant he had been unable to reply earlier. "But that's surely not a problem, as I'm accepting now". "Sorry", came the unexpected answer, "but it's too late". "Well put me down for next year then. At once!"

As a consolation for those of you who did not get invited, I can reveal that you can actually treat yourself to a real Nobel dinner. You do not need an invitation, but a table reservation at the City Hall Restaurant would be advisable. You will then be served the complete menu on the Nobel dinner service, with wines and all. You can even choose among menus from previous years, but then the kitchen needs some warning so that the right ingredients can be acquired.

One menu has turned out to be particularly popular, above all with Japanese tourists visiting Sweden. In 1994, the Literature Prize went to Oe Kenzaburo and by the autumn of 2000, a total of 24,000 guests – most of them Japanese – had eaten the same dinner that Japan's great son received on that occasion. More than once, the headwaiter has been tentatively asked whether it would be possible to have the food served on the same platter that was used to serve Mr Oe.

TO THE TABLE • Back to the Blue Hall, where by now the guests have had time to admire the details of the well-laid table and the decorations, in the form of flowers and otherwise. The evening's first procession of actors is now making its entrance the same way the guests of honour have just trod. It is the 50 wine waiters, who have had their bottles opened by 6 cork pullers. The latter are important persons with the special task of opening the many bottles that will appear on the tables during the evening. The wine waiters, with their bottles of chilled champagne in a firm grip, now proceed down the stairs and out among the tables. I am always just as impressed to see the precision of these waiters. The very best vista is probably from the commentator's box up on the balcony outside the Golden Hall,

where we were based during the television broadcasts. From up there, you have a birds-eye view of everything that happens down in the Blue Hall, including the restaurateur's exceedingly discreet signal to start serving the champagne. The solemnity of the first toast is such that it is almost tangible, and that toast is to the King. The sound of 5,200 chair legs being pulled back across the marble floor is not one that can be justly conveyed through a modest loudspeaker, it has to be experienced on the spot! The sound level and its myriad of variations during the dinner would incidentally suffice to provide material for a mammoth doctoral thesis on acoustics. I dread to think how it may have sounded in the 1970s, when the meal was still served in the Golden Hall. There was admittedly 'only' room

For those who cannot leave the kitchen during the evening, the Nobel Banquet next door does not become real until seen on the TV screen.

for 600-700 guests, but the acoustics were grotesque, and I am expressing myself diplomatically.

As with most really grand occasions, it is possible to plot a graph showing the increase in exhilaration during this banquet. At first, the guests behave with academic reserve and dignity, but as the evening wears on, the mood takes flight and formality cedes to unrestrained festivity. But the way the evening unfolds in detail is something that the guests can never guess in advance. Although perhaps, television broadcasts from previous Nobel banquets can give some idea of what could occur.

Over the years, television coverage of the festivities in the City Hall has naturally changed character. In the early 1970s, the management of Swedish Television (SVT) was still living in the shadow of the events of 1968 and radical student protest, and this had its influence on what they considered viewers' licence fees should be spent on. To televise a lengthy academic dinner with some speeches in the City Hall was not one of their top priorities, and Channel 1 – the senior channel – considered one year that all the resources should be reserved for a music festival, so it was the new Channel 2 that was 'landed' with the Nobel. But the internal SVT status associated with the broadcast was low, to say the least, until the Nobel Foundation contacted an American TV company. With such competition lurking round the corner, SVT suddenly pulled its socks up. As research and science issues began to acquire a certain degree of glamour, it was realized that something special ought to be made of the ceremony so that the whole event radiated splendour. And that this splendour could attract the media which of course increased the media coverage, and then the snowball effect was a fact. Greater interest thus demanded increased television resources, and more television led to increased interest.

But the fact remained, something had to be done about the

design of both the banquet and the way it was presented on television. For the Managing Director of the Nobel Foundation, Mr Stig Ramel, it was a question of 'more haste, less speed'. The Academies were sensitive about rapid changes, and the Foundation must under no circumstances find itself suspected of rash management of the economic resources. In the reform process, Ramel found an ally in the then Crown Prince, Carl Gustaf, whom he had served in an earlier position in the office of the Comptroller of the Royal Household.

A movement had been made in the direction of shaping the event which would work well on television, at a time when an ever-increasing number of features were vying for viewers' time and interest. Television tries to satisfy the public's 'expected expectations', in as much as it is possible to do so. A method that 'my' producer, Mr Torbjörn Olausson, tried, was to 'depart from' the actual course of events, and instead record selected parts and then use these later in the evening. To forget 'real time' and extemporize. The ambition was to cut away the parts that might not have seemed long to the participants, but that lost their effect when seen on the screen. To turn a private party into an entertaining as well as an informative television programme.

At the planning stage, this can seem like a hopeless task. Again came the question, what would interest the person who chooses to follow the evening via his television set? We can perhaps compare this with other major events involving television. A football cup final, or a symphony concert from a famous concert hall in some international venue. The distance to the football stadium or the fact that the tickets are sold-out, can mean that we are unable to be there in person. We have to rely on a relayed report of the whole thing, and that means that somebody other than the viewer chooses which parts are to be included, and how they are going to be shown. A person who is physically present can freely concentrate on what seems

interesting around him. He might thus look away from what is happening on centre stage, and find his attention caught by somebody's beautiful clothes or details in the furnishings. As a viewer, you have to give up that freedom, but you get something very valuable in return.

What I have in mind is the close-up. The ability of the camera to shorten distance and serve as a sharp, enlarging eye. It is a moment's work to move us from one side of the hall to the other side, and land within reach of what is just happening, far away. A close-up makes us participants in the action. Although we are seated firmly and comfortably in our armchairs at home, we are nevertheless sitting next to the Chairman of the Nobel Foundation at the same moment he proposes a toast to His Majesty the King. And the same close-up lets us slip past all the security men and come so close to the King that we can count the bubbles in his champagne glass when His Majesty in turn proposes a toast to Alfred Nobel two minutes later.

How many of the guests in the expanse of the Blue Hall can count on having such a good vantage point that they can switch between a birds-eye view and the detailed intimacy of a close-up? Not a single one! On an evening like this, television can show what it is really capable of. The ability to take us to where things are happening right now, but without us having to leave our armchairs. The possibility of choosing, and choosing to ignore. The possibility of skimming off the cream in the form of beautiful pictures and getting to know somebody intimately. What we in the television team hoped to do, was to be able to reflect a long, solemn banqueting celebration, its speeches, and its dancing, so that the viewer felt as though he or she had been invited and was welcome. We tried to compress those parts of the evening that seemed rather long-winded, break up what seemed monotonous on a television screen, and with the help of several visits 'behind the scenes' push the plot – and thereby the viewer too – along.

For the seven years from 1987 to 1993, that I had the pleasure of being the viewers' voice and eye in the City Hall, much of the challenge lay in precisely the possibility of discovering variations in a regular banqueting event, where the main features remain the same year after year. And many we were, who shared in that hunt: the planners with their ideas, the chefs and the wine connoisseurs with theirs, and of course the designers of the framework, the processions, the displays. Art historian Åke Livstedt was a member of the '90th jubilee think-tank' in 1991 which concerned itself with renewing the ceremonies and their rôle during the evening. One of his ideas in the quest to achieve a logical location for the entertainment, was to try to incorporate it in what was already happening in the way of movements and logistical arrangements in and around the Blue Hall. The point was also that the entertainment should not rudely interrupt all the conversation at the tables in an abrupt manner. For that matter, it is not the easiest thing in the world to cut off the animated conversations of 1,300 people and get them all to direct their attention to one solitary entertainer.

So when do the longueurs occur in a dinner like this? When each course is cleared away. Glasses and crockery must be removed and replaced, and various odds and ends moved around, and this can even be a little noisy too. There are lots of people round and about the guests and it is essential that they all know how the 'traffic' should flow to avoid jams and crashes.

What the organizers did was to examine if it would be possible to make these various movements more effective. Perhaps some time could be saved? Time that could be used in a more constructive manner. They had an apparatus to count steps, and a stop-watch too, and gradually worked out a completely new 'flowchart' for the army of waiters and waitresses. But the fact remained – valuable time still ran away when the food was

The ice-cream procession on its way down the marble staircase in the Blue Hall.

being served and the dishes cleared away. So the 'think-tank' proposed turning this into an asset by letting it become entertainment. After all, the conversation tends to quieten down at these moments, and the guests are ready for surprises.

The Baroque period was a time of great gestures, in all respects. Music, clothing and not least food and processions. In 1649 a magnificent Peace banquet was held to celebrate the end of the Thirty Years' War. We still have some etchings which show in detail what this grandiose dinner looked like, with its imposing processions and intricately constructed platters of food. Would it be possible to put some of the Baroque ideas into practice today, to have the magnificence of the Baroque in the modern setting of today's Nobel anniversary dinner?

Looking back, many commentators now see that 1991 was a major turning point when it came to artistic creativity in a Nobel Banquet context. The separate entertainment features that slowed down the evening, these were removed from the programme. In their place, came integrated elements which did not steal time in the same way. Maybe some of the regular guests did not feel completely at home in the unadorned, rather bare Blue Hall. No flowers, no standing decorations were to be seen when the evening commenced. Everything was to be successively brought in as an integral part of the dinner itself.

During the Renaissance, it was the custom to use dancers when one wanted to create a specially festive entry procession. That idea was applicable here too, and to realize it the Foundation called upon Mr Ivo Cramér, choreographer and ballet master with a genuine interest in the formal dances of olden times. His dancers came from the Swedish Ballet School, young people with stage experience who could rapidly adapt themselves to the new ideas that were hatched. Ivo's choreographed entrances elegantly solved a number of problems: it

was the dancers who brought in the flowers and the decorative elements when they came down to the guests at the tables. To the beat of drums and the sound of trumpets, the staircase came alive with colour when the dancers carried in tall white amaryllises, and large green leaf decorations. In their wake, the first course was brought in: nettle soup which symbolized spring and the continent of America. Waiters and waitresses had also all been given some elementary choreographic instruction by ballet master Cramér, so that the procession music should be 'seen' in their bodies. Throughout the entire dinner, a playfully applied theme – around the number 'four' – was repeatedly in evidence: the four seasons, the four classic continents, the four basic prizes and the four colours on the rims of the plates. A delight for the eye, and greatly appreciated by the guests.

But processions and movements need some space, and many of the theatrical elements we have seen over the years, would not have been feasible at all if the dinner had not been moved from the Golden Hall to the Blue Hall in 1974. That move opened up all sorts of new opportunities, and the guests of honour could now make their joint and magnificent entrance along the balcony and down the stairs. The importance of the staircase should not be underestimated, because it provided a brilliant stage, be it for entrances, performances or speeches. Many are the hazardous tricks that have been performed by artistes who have realized what possibilities are created by the steeply inclined, broad and massive banisters.

The move downstairs was also a blessing to the caterers, who could now use the enormous area of the Golden Hall to prepare and cook the dish that was next in turn to be carried down to the guests. The food was now close by, and some of those vexatious transports along long corridors are now a thing of the past. On television we are used to seeing the Golden Hall filled with dancing couples, later in the evening, but during the dinner it is like a central command station. Long tables stand side-by-side, heavily laden with platters. Large steel pots with piping hot sauces, straight from the kitchens, are placed here. And this is where the final garnishing and various trimmings are added. A last check is made that everyone knows his or her place in the procession, and the mood is one of efficiency and exhilaration in sweet union. Friendly jokes are exchanged among the staff, but should the time schedule be seriously threatened, then everyone sharpens up.

The conversing guests down below, notice none of this activity while they are waiting for the first course to be served. This dinner has only just begun, and there is plenty of time to find subjects to discuss, and just as much time to worry if you have nothing to say. It is impossible, although admittedly rather fascinating, to try to imagine what sort of things are discussed down there among the guests. The mass of voices, which gets louder as the evening progresses, makes it impossible to eavesdrop. But the body language of the conversing guests can give some clues as to how well they are coping with the situation. From my observation post up on the balcony, I can easily watch the evening's festively attired company, without being seen myself. As at all parties, the 'take-off run' varies from guest to guest. Some start off right away, and put a great deal of energy into laying the foundations for a nice evening with his or her partner. Others are more cautious, they wait and hope that the solemn atmosphere will disappear of its own accord. Still others seem ravenously hungry and waiting for the food. Some are on the look-out for famous faces, while others again seem to think that their salvation will be the dance after about a further three hours in a chair which is already feeling rather too familiar…

This is the moment of truth. Is the ever so carefully planned seating arrangement a success? A party arranger can never know for sure whether all the guests have been satisfied

with their placing. On one occasion, an academic gentleman complained not about his own placing, but about a colleague's. The objection was that his colleague had evidently been given a 'finer' placing than he himself had!

Guests should still have a little champagne left in their glasses, after the two toasts so far proposed. The champagne is usually of the best sort, and comes from one of the great houses – which one gets the honour, varies. The guest must try to strike a delicate balance between the desire to empty his glass while the content is still more or less at the right temperature, and rationing until the first course wine arrives. A combination of etiquette and waiting-time usually solves the problem and when the first course is carried in, many guests may be seen discreetly emptying their champagne glass.

Nowadays, it is not only an interest in food and cooking that is very popular, but also wine-tasting and wine clubs mean that many of the evening's guests will be keenly awaiting the selection of wines to be served. The choice is not made until the menu is finalized; first then, can the search begin for suitable wines. For many years, French wines were the obvious choice, but in the early 1990s the organizers started looking further afield, even towards the New World. At the same time, the maximum limit of what a wine could cost, was raised, so that the list of potential wines was greatly enlarged, and the wine-tasting sessions also acquired new proportions. Several members of the Nobel Foundation are gourmets and wine experts, and they take an active part in the tastings. Of course, the choice of menu restricts which types of wines are considered. Food and wine must be suited to each other, or 'married' in terms of taste, and as the dishes often contain several different ingredients, with varying degrees of saltness, acidity or strength of taste, the choice of wine is not an easy one. And there is no shortage of wine houses only too ready to see their name figure in connection with the Nobel Banquet.

For one of our broadcasts, we visited the wine cellar of the City Hall Restaurant. Like most wine cellars, this is rather cramped and much smaller than one might expect a treasure trove for fine wines to be. But there, in the glare of naked light bulbs, were stacked sufficient bottles of varied vintage to excite even the most indifferent visitor. This applied even to the wines that were served with the dessert. In earlier years, the organizers had relied heavily on port wine, but as the hunt for new table wines became all the more intense, even in this case they started to look afresh at old hunting grounds. In recent years, the dessert has often been accompanied by French products, the great, very rich wines from Sauternes. Or just as often a German or Austrian Beerenauslese, where the grapes have been laboriously sorted by hand, one by one, to ripen until their taste inclines towards the smoothness of honey. Or even a step up in quality, Trockenbeerenauslese with its exquisite taste. These wines can only be produced in exceptional years, and this is reflected in the price. But in the Nobel glass the guest is then served a fairly weak wine the taste of which often overwhelms with its richness. The old faithful from Madeira is appreciated by many connoisseurs, but that wine is regrettably not particularly 'modern' nowadays, as is witnessed by the declining import statistics. A renaissance may be on the way, but hardly in the context of the Nobel Banquet, partly because the desserts often contain some sort of sorbet with plenty of naturally fruity acidity, and in such cases the Madeira loses its powers of contrast with regard to the food.

It may seem a pleasant task for those responsible for the wine, to have so many types to choose from, but it is not at all easy. Every year, about fifteen guests inform the Foundation that they would like a non-alcoholic alternative throughout the meal. This is usually due to the customs in the guest's home

The Royalties and the other guests of honour, are the first to leave the table.

When the guests have risen from the table of honour, all the other guests can tread the well-laid steps in Ragnar Östberg's magnificent stairway.

country, or a deliberate choice to abstain from any stimulant substances.

Let us not get lost in speculation as to why one particular dessert wine ends up on the table this evening, and not another. The armada, clad in white, approaches the tables and then gathers up the empty champagne glasses. A few moments of comparative calm, before music or lights cause those assembled to look towards the staircase and balcony. For the commanders in the Golden Hall, it is now too late to ask if everything is ready. It simply has to be, and there is only one possibility: to give the signal to a new armada of waiters and waitresses to find their platters and bottles and form up ready to carry forth the first course.

Just like at a big theatre performance, the director has tried to anticipate and remove reasons that may cause things to go wrong. The day before, all the waiters and waitresses have rehearsed their part in the procession, following exactly the same route they will take during the banquet. Although there was one important difference: the large platters were empty, and the balance was of course not the same as it would be if they were fully laden. At this rehearsal, there was a mixture of old hands and younger, curious newcomers, and several times I could not help but be reminded of the joyful expectation preceding a school outing. I do not of course know whether these 'schoolmates' were exchanging tales of catastrophes with dropped platters, but it is surely not completely unthinkable. And just by naming the worst possible scenario, it becomes less terrifying. If you can 'tempt the troll out into the sunshine', he will start to disintegrate – or so the fairy tale goes.

Many of the staff serving on this remarkable evening, also work in the City Hall in their everyday job. Large dinners, banquets and private parties are all a part of their day-to-day work, where a natural part of their professional pride is the art of being extroverted. The cameras' many shots of individuals and personalities reveal faces reflecting the expectations of the public, the way dancers do in a theatre. Once out on the staircase, it is hardly appropriate to look down to see where to tread; just like a dancer, their feet must find their own way. And nor must it show, that it can be quite exhausting to carry the well-filled platters. Again just like for a dancer, any effort has to be hidden behind a smile. And perhaps that smile will be more natural this evening, when the wave of warmth and energy from the 1,300 guests is almost tangible. When the waiters and waitresses are finally in place out among the tables, it is always equally fascinating to watch how they discreetly, almost imperceptibly, look out for the restaurateur's similarly discreet signal. The King and Queen are served a few moments before the other guests, and out of reach of the microphones you can sometimes observe them passing comments on what has just been served.

As television viewers, we are used to all those cooking programmes where we get a close-up view of all the dishes, so that we can see, for example, sugar peas filling an entire 28 inch screen! In such programmes, nothing is left to chance, the lighting is well thought-out and the food is often brushed with oil so that it will look really fresh. When our reporting team occasionally was let into the City Hall kitchens to see how the chefs were preparing the evening's menu, there was no time to direct and re-arrange everything for the Perfect Picture. The chefs had their hands full, the powerful strip lights in the ceiling sabotaged every attempt at delicate illumination, and the noise of the steel pots and machines was always loudly present. But once we did in fact manage to have a couple of place settings arranged on a table in the Golden Hall in advance. The chef's description of the various ingredients was full of feeling, and he described their taste, and how he and his colleagues had discussed the menu and all its constituent parts so that the final result would be balance and harmony. I was drawn all the

The strict formal dress of the male guests this evening, allows the ladies' magnificent gowns to blossom in full.

deeper into a discussion about salinity and saturation, contrasts and highlighted flavours, and all with a vocabulary which could more than match that of a wine taster. It was not until it was all over and the dishes had been cleared away that I realized I had forgotten the most important of all – to decipher the chef's elegant 'food-French' and explain to the viewer in ordinary Swedish what we actually had seen on the platters. Yes, well… wind down the curtain!

While the guests are busy with their first course, we in the reporting team take the opportunity to try to identify selected guests from our vantage point up on the balcony along one long side of the Blue Hall. The little 'seating booklet' is a reliable guide, to help us localize – and then capture on camera – the celebrities we want to talk about. The simplest is of course the 'heart', the table that is the centre of the hall, the table with the laureates and the guests of honour. And every year, the actors at that table have to resign themselves to being upstaged by the Queen. It is around her that all the photographers tend to flock, they all want pictures of the jewels round her neck and the gems in her hair. For my own part, being the grandson of a theatre tailor at the Royal Opera House, I was interested in describing the cloth and cut of the magnificent creations worn by the Queen. But you could not plan this in advance. It was often not known until the last minute what had been chosen in the Palace, but we usually got word of this from a breathless messenger just in time for our broadcast.

The same goes for the evening's jewels, which had of course to harmonize with the colours and lustre of the evening gown. The extremely detailed close-ups that the television cameramen shot of the magnificent jewels looked very good on screen, and must have elicited a gasp or two from jewellery experts. But it felt a little like we were planning an advanced jewellery robbery, when we and the viewers studied the rarities in such detail.

When we let the camera slowly pan along the rows of guests at the head table, we tried to provide a little background for some of the individuals thus portrayed. There was no difficulty in obtaining information about the evening's main actors, the laureates, who had already been bled white by the various media in the weeks preceding the ceremony. The challenge lay in using just a few sentences to sketch a picture of the person behind the discovery that had rendered him or her one of the prizes. It was just as rewarding to try to portray a laureate's wife, who was strikingly often a personality in her own right with a decidedly interesting life. That rather hackneyed phrase about there being a woman behind every great man, did not seem to apply when we looked at the laureates' wives or fiancées. They were doctors, researchers and entrepreneurs, women with demanding work and unusual hobbies. It was not quite as easy to find exciting details about the guests from government and diplomatic circles, who returned year after year.

An obvious subject of conversation at a banquet on this scale, is of course the way the guests are dressed. And I do not refer to the gentlemen, whose tail coats are similar in style and cut from year to year, to put it mildly. And any medals and orders that they may be sporting, are soon described, so the interest is naturally concentrated upon the ladies' evening gowns. The variety is great, the models are many, and the choice of colour may well often be a result of a desire to set off all the black-and-white gentlemen. One who succeeded perfectly in that respect, was the wife of the French ambassador. When we had her in picture, the contrast filter indicator on our monitors almost went over the top! Her dress was nothing but gold, the cut was brilliant and it was worn with grace. The Swedish Minister of Education by her side, looked like a timid grey mouse in comparison…

It was a superb move of the 'think tank' behind the 1991

anniversary banquet to merge together the serving of the food with the entertainment, in line with the old Baroque prescription of entries and processions. It was never a question of slavishly copying a 17th century banquet, although the old records make fascinating reading with their descriptions of wild excesses. There is mention of clouds of birds that flew up out of enormous pies, and desserts with pyrotechnic displays that would cause a modern fire safety officer to age ten years in thirty seconds.

Guests in our day have been able to enjoy several years' of processions marked by beauty and richness of colour, while the serving of the various courses has become quicker and more flowing then before. The lessons of these years have been learnt well, and now the time schedule for movements and table-laying or clearing is so pared down, that there is little room for improvement.

THE SPEECHES • Great dinners mean, of course, speeches of varying content and length. And on this particular evening, the laureates have had plenty of practice in the preceding weeks, during which they have been the prey of the media. They have talked of their discoveries in the most serious journals and the most frivolous tabloids. They have gone into great detail and they have popularized, and as a layman I think they deserve to be able to relax and simply enjoy all the beauty around them. However it is customary for a representative for each prize to make a little speech some time in the evening. If the prize is shared, then the most senior laureate has the honour and speaks on behalf of his colleague(s). Now at last, the chosen few can ignore the formal approach, and resort to all the spontaneity and humour they are capable of. A submissive, sitting audience of giant proportions, is hanging on their lips, and the television cameras register the slightest shift of expression in the speaker's face. As in life in general, people are

Sometimes, the arts and politics go hand in hand.
Gudrun Schyman of the Left Party and Sven Wollter, actor.

very different. Where one person is completely natural in the company of others, another may feel it embarrassing to be stared at. Some are spurred on to great deeds, and celebrate triumphs in the higher school of rhetoric, while others say what has to be said and want to leave the podium as soon as possible. The latter category has one excellent characteristic: they do not exceed their allotted time; indeed, they are nearly always finished sooner than planned. The former category can be a problem. If they meet with a warm reception, and some laughter from down among the tables, there is a risk that the speaker's imagination may flow a little too freely. The written speech is added to, and new sidetracks acquire a life of their own while time slips by. This has sometimes meant that an already long dinner has touched the outer limits of the broadcasting time… and of people's patience. Not least out of consideration of television schedules, an urgent recommendation was put forward to restrict each speech to a maximum of five minutes. This request first met with surprise among the Nobel organizers. Restrict the speeches of the laureates – the very thought! But after further discussion, agreement was reached, and since then there have been many five-minute speeches that have served as refreshing elements towards the end of the dinner. On one occasion, however, even five minutes multiplied by the number of laureates, was too much for one of the poor students who had been holding a ceremonial standard beside the podium. The student and his standard fell to the floor together, the press photographers scented blood and there were lots of flashes as the unfortunate student was helped up by his comrades. Our cameras were focussed upon the current speaker, whose words were both interesting and spiced with humour, so we refrained from showing the intermezzo with the swooning student. The evening papers did not refrain, however, and they portrayed the fallen hero in greater dimensions than that year's laureates. Unfortunately, the bosses in the television centre had the same opinion as to what was newsworthy, and we were sharply criticized for missing what they considered to be the 'scoop of the year'!

THE DESERT COURSE • To return to the subject of the processions, it does not really matter how they will come to be formed at future banquets. But one procession is absolutely bound to return year after year in some form or other. I have in mind the ice-cream parade. After the laureates and the Queen, it is the entry of the dessert that most seems to fascinate people. Any other dessert is quite as unthinkable, as the reputation of the Nobel ice-cream is firmly established. The parade down the stairs in the darkened Blue Hall is exactly the same every year. But that is not true of the ice cream itself. Anyone able to read the culinary French of the menu, can work out in advance just which tastes the ice-cream makers have played with. "Glace d'épices et sorbet à l'ananas avec compôte de fruits de la passion et d'ananas". That was 1999. Or why not go back four years earlier: "Parfait Nobel en voile sorbet aux baies d'archipel et son parfait vanille". My kingdom for a pocket French dictionary! The magnificent extravagance of the Baroque advances one stop closer our own time with these words, and both appetite and expectation are at their peak already before the meal has started.

For many years this cherished dessert was a fancy ice-cream gâteau with some fruit to taste, the whole being crowned with an 'N' in golden brown caramel. But inventive professionals with creative talents could add something new even to such an 'institution', and soon all sorts of imaginative creations started to appear. The platters were suddenly filled with models that let a whole little symphony orchestra of different, pure tastes surge forth on your palate, opening up like a Gothic church arch in amazement. Every year saw new experiments with sorbets and parfaits, in addition to the basic ice-cream.

Now, all tastes could be incorporated in the ice-cream construction, and I do not exaggerate when I compare this to a building site. Because many detailed drawings were made of the planned model-of-the-year in cross section, where the various tastes were so placed as to ensure that both harmony and contrast could come into play. You do not need to read French to be tempted, English will do quite nicely. One year, the guests were served an outer shell of black current parfait which encased a kernel of elder flower and passion fruit sorbet. Round the base of the gâteau was candy floss, small pieces of chocolate with various fillings and delicate almond biscuits. The whole creation was crowned with a caramel letter 'N'.

This simple letter has an almost unbelievable status in this context, comparable only with big game on the African savannah! It is most rare to be able to discover an intact 'N' on the platters with melting ice-cream which are carried out after the guests have left the tables. So where do they end up? Some are no doubt taken by the children that accompany some of the laureates, and who find here a delicious, sweet end to a long sitting at table. But where the others disappear to, is of course a more worrying question. This caramel creation arrives at the tables crisply cold on the top of the ice gâteau, but it gradually warms up, like everything else in the hall. Anybody who has ever left a caramel in his pocket, knows what it feels like when he comes across it later. So I think we can exclude pockets from our list, and not just because of the stickiness factor. This is really quite a large 'N' and it would certainly get broken into smaller pieces, impossible to put together again at home. So unfortunately there remains but one alternative: the elegant ladies' evening vanity bag. However tiny and delicate such a golden or silver bag may be, there always seems to be room for this trophy together with the lipstick and powder compact. The next interesting question is: When is the act committed, and how? I can only try to emulate the best television detectives' working methods, and put forward a number of theories in the hunt for the missing letter. The kitchen staff can certify that there are never any broken caramel remains among the melted ice-cream on the platters when they come back, which ought to indicate that the letter has not been shared out fairly among the guests at the table. So there is reason to suspect that one person has taken the letter, perhaps aided and abetted by an accomplice. And has this happened with an amusing aside, or was it done surreptitiously? Does the guest look entreatingly at the waitress just before the platter leaves the table? There are many questions, but the answers are enveloped in mystery. And what actually happens with the 'N' if it manages to be appropriated in one piece by its new owner? As opposed to the big game of the savannah, it can hardly be stuffed and hung on the wall in the drawing room. Perhaps some of them are nevertheless consumed in the normal way during the course of the evening.

Some restaurants amuse themselves by sometimes offering ice-cream 'à la Nobel' among their desserts. But this nearly always means that the dessert, whatever it looks like, is crowned with glittering sparklers. At the City Hall, nobody can ever remember having sparklers in the gâteaux, which would actually add to the multitude of flavours with that of iron filings. However, the organizers' imaginations have been allowed to run wild in the hunt for festive effects in connection with the ice-cream procession. On one occasion they wanted to serve ice-cream lying on a block of ice, which was not quite as easy as they expected it to be. A lump of ice has a tendency to slide about on a serving platter, and should it have a highly-built ice-cream gâteau on top of it, then it could well turn into an

(Opposite page) The Queen of Lake Mälaren in gold mosaic, looks down from the short wall in the Golden Hall, upon the dance which is sometimes courteous and sometimes rather wild.

unpredictable projectile! A damp tea towel between the platter and the ice block, solved that problem, and they could go on to reflect as to how they could arrange some sort of lighting effect from inside the block of ice. The blocks were frozen with a hole in the middle to house a light source. But what could be used? Light bulbs and batteries were all very well, but if that combination went on strike at the crucial moment, this would constitute a fiasco. But here too, help was at hand from an unexpected quarter. The Swedish navy use a special type of emergency flare which once activated provides plenty of illumination for a short time. The flare fitted nicely in the ice block, and the effect when the ice-cream procession entered the darkened hall was brilliant.

But if we see the evening in general as an opportunity to display Sweden for an international audience, then not even the most spectacular ice-cream procession will long suffice as entertainment. Round about the time of the dessert, there are expectations that something should happen, and in the late 1980s the organizers begin to reflect upon how the entertainment could be built up with Swedish artistes. One year, television people suggested using a young musician, Miss Åsa Jinder, one of the best players of traditional stringed instruments in the country. The idea was that she should stand in one of the windows opposite the balcony in the Blue Hall, and play something that was undisputedly Swedish. Åsa was amazed to be asked, but she accepted and after rehearsals on the afternoon of the 10th, everyone was satisfied. A young musician in folk costume playing an unusual traditional instrument – that ought to remain fixed in the guests' memory once and for all.

The evening came, and when the ice-cream had been paraded out among the tables, Åsa put her bow to the instrument and started to play. She could hear what she played; we could hear in our headphones and via the monitors what she played. But the guests at the tables could hardly hear her at all. On

account of some fatal misunderstanding, our sound system was not on the same wavelength as the one in the City Hall, and many of the conversations at the tables continued with unabated intensity. For the television broadcast, everything went as planned, and, despite the mistake, this performance did in fact contribute to new ideas as regards the entertainment at the banquet.

MIXING • When the dessert and the coffee have been enjoyed, it is time to make a move. The guests have already been sitting for between three and four hours, and it is certainly a pleasure to be able to stretch one's legs a little, and follow the Royal Family and the guests of honour as they make their way up the stairs towards the Golden Hall. Most of the guests now begin to move around spontaneously, chat to acquaintances, make new contacts.

This is of course a completely unique occasion to make informal contacts. The type of contacts, which not many will admit openly, but which often nevertheless seem to lie behind many plans and successful projects. Such as tentative proposals made on the golf course – that is just how it feels amid the conversations after the Nobel Banquet. The Swedish attitude to new technology is characterised by curiosity, and Stockholm has received a number of international awards as a leading IT centre and as a meeting place for different interests. So there is plenty for the foreign guests to talk about, during the banquet as well as the rest of the Nobel week, much of which is decidedly informal. I have in mind all those occasions when young researchers are given the opportunity to meet the laureates out of reach of the media. It may be in the form of lectures or seminars, or even early in the morning at the laureates' hotel with a Lucia Parade. When the festivities are over, there are plans for a Nobel Museum to meet around. The City Hall Restaurant's Nobel menu is on offer all the year, and reminds

the summer tourists, Swedish as well as foreign, of the winter event. In a time when it is a case of being seen amid the masses, then Nobel is without doubt a trade mark in a class all on its own. In the year 2002, Stockholm will celebrate its 750th anniversary, and it will be interesting to see how Nobel will contribute to the festivities.

But not everybody has time for informal contacts at this stage of the evening. For a limited number of guests, with the laureates and their families first, it is now time for what may well seem the highlight of the evening. Inside the beautiful, long and narrow Prince's Gallery (named after Prince Eugen, the artist prince of Waldemarsudde), the King and Queen receive the chosen guests, and the photograph from this occasion will for many be proof that they have once in their lives managed to speak with a real King and his Consort.

THE DANCE • To be responsible for a major 'one-off' event could make anyone nervous. There is nothing to compare with and lean on from previous occasions; everything has to be done from scratch for this one time. But that can also be a blessing in disguise. Nobody knows exactly what has been planned and the guests can only judge on the basis of what they themselves have experienced. But if it is a regular event, there are lots of opinions already registered and everybody has a view as to how the thing should be arranged to achieve the best possible result. The organizers then find themselves deciding whether to retain or change parts of the programme. If they take away something that the public is used to, so that it is no longer "the same as it always used to be", then someone will nearly always raise a protest. It is a delicate matter to replace 'old faithfuls', but sometimes it has to be done.

THE MUSIC • For anybody charged with arranging a banquet, one of the most tricky tasks must be that of finding

After a few dances, some of the guests return to the calm of the Blue Hall.

"Well, I say…" Princess Lilian makes a surprising discovery together with Elisabeth Palmstierna and Alice Trolle-Wachtmeister.

the ideal dance orchestra. Nothing can puncture a carefully built-up festive atmosphere as effectively as a badly chosen orchestra. And the Nobel evening is a challenge for any orchestra, because the public can hardly be said to be homogenous. There are all sorts of eager dancers, from students who have only just realized that you can actually hold your partner when you dance, to elderly worthies who are glad to have somebody to hang on to! So how should the music be chosen, so that each and everyone will feel that the evening has been rounded off with a jolly atmosphere?

Well, nobody masters the art of making absolutely everybody happy, but you can come pretty close if you start by ruling out options that simply will not work. A rock group would hardly please a majority, and nor would a jazz band. A tango orchestra might well be appreciated by a certain category but otherwise the dance floor would remain sparsely populated. The solution would seem to lie close to a sort of 'qualified lowest common denominator' which is: an orchestra whose repertoire covers a large variety of styles of dance music, and can even take in its stride the requests that suddenly may turn up at short notice.

Over the years, orchestras have come and gone, and musical taste has varied in the Golden Hall. In the late 1980s, it was time for some new ideas, and Stig Ramel suggested to the television producer Torbjörn Olausson that they ought to look for an orchestra that 'played like Lester Lanin'. It transpired that Lanin was the leader of the American musicians who regularly provided the musical accompaniment at state banquets and other ceremonious occasions. Naturally, the orchestra played very well, but it also had another unusual quality. It could adjust its repertoire to the mood in the dance hall. That might sound somewhat banal, and ought perhaps to go without saying. But how often can you honestly say that you have come across an orchestra that seems to feel the 'vibes' and knows exactly which tune will get things going? No desperate searching, but the next tune seems to fall into place like a well sawn-out piece in a jigsaw puzzle. Unfortunately, Lester Lanin and his men tended to be on tour in America, so somebody had to be found here in Sweden. The first choice was Leif Kronlund's orchestra, which meant that nearly everybody spent some time on the dance floor the next two years. In their wake followed other ensembles, but the spirit of Lester Lanin's flexible orchestra still seemed to hold sway.

And a good thing too, because the Nobel Ball in the Golden Hall is attended by all sorts of guests of widely varying ages. And it was fun to be the television commentator and look out over this surging sea of people, and note all the styles of dancing in practice. Students with lots of energy who jumped about like joyful Muppets. Academic personages with orders round their necks who danced in a strict and dignified manner. And Swedish celebrities with their never-failing skill at manoeuvring self and partner to a position right in front of our cameras. And then of course all the others who were simply having a really good time to the tones of old favourites and new, heady Latin rhythms.

THE INTERVIEWS • In order to broadcast the evening's events from the City Hall, a great deal of planning is necessary. Looking back, I understood that there were two aspects. Firstly, what was possible to work out in advance and give some structure to, and secondly, what happened during the evening that was outside our (or anybody else's) control. I ought to say at once, that most things could be anticipated, the course of the evening was a sort of skeleton which gave the direction and times in an approximate manner. But then we have reality, which sometimes seems to live an infuriating life of its own.

There is nothing simple about broadcasting from the City Hall. To start with, it is a gigantic building and the practical

Mr and Mrs Jacob Wallenberg – caught on camera.

side of things with running all the cables from the buses up through the window openings, along the ventilation shafts, in stairwells and corridors – that alone was a mammoth job. And then the festivities take place on different levels, which makes it difficult to position the various cameras so that we can quickly be where the action is. In the 1980s, hand-held cameras were not good enough so that they could replace the heavy studio cameras, which took up a great deal of space with their large tripods on castors. On several occasions, I saw our studio man come rushing along, with his arms clearing the way for one of these cameras with cameraman and crew trying to push aside the stiff, red cables so that the nearby guests would not become ensnared.

And it might sound rather obvious, but to be able to ensure that such a major television broadcast succeeds, it is necessary to have a stable supply of electricity. A Nobel Banquet is not a candlelight dinner, even if there are plenty of candelabras on the tables. On this evening the whole building is lit up with all manner of lamps and chandeliers, straining the electrical system of the City Hall to its utmost. And it becomes even more lit-up when all the television equipment is turned on, inside the building and outside too. One year, the old wiring and fuse-boxes just could not cope, and the broadcast started with a completely blank screen. After what seemed like an eternity, the whole system started up again and I could welcome viewers to that year's Nobel Banquet. But the year after, we took along our own generator and there were no more such mishaps.

Another detail which turned out to require very special planning, were my attempts at interviewing laureates we were particularly interested in. It is one thing to sit in your office and dream about this or that person, but actually getting hold of them on the evening itself is quite another matter.

The Nobel Foundation invites all the laureates, and their

Be it Cinderella's ball or the Nobel Banquet – they all come to an end.

families, to a special party at the Old Stock Exchange on the 9th of December. This provides an excellent opportunity to approach the people we wished to interview. But the hall is so crowded with guests, surging and pressing forward around tables laden with dainty sandwiches, chocolates and champagne. A combination of stubbornness, diplomacy and sheer strength was needed to get at the big game and their families. But even if this succeeded, there was no actual guarantee that the interview so eagerly awaited 24 hours later would actually come off. Because there were always others who wanted to come and lighten their hearts for the by then rather exhausted laureates, who had done little else but answer questions, and had been doing so for several days in a row.

But their ordeal was not yet over, and with admirable patience they listened to us and our plans for where and how we would arrange our little chat when the dinner was finally over. "And what do you want to know, then?" I explained that it was not particularly interesting at this stage to go yet again through the discovery that had led to the prize. That had already filled the papers for weeks, and had been described in detail and from all possible angles in specialist, as well as popular, magazines. As I had been educated in the humanities, it also remained doubtful that I would have been able to make complex scientific processes any more intelligible for the viewers, so I decided at an early stage to adopt another strategy. What was the person like, concealed behind the formal starched white shirt? It did not seem unreasonable to assume that we would meet replete and relaxed laureates who had done enough talking about their own discoveries. It would be late in the evening, and the party spirit would surely be an ally as we tried to get under their skin. During the short and rather noisy conversations at the Stock Exchange, I tried to form – if not a picture, then at least a sketch, of the personality behind the researcher.

During my first Nobel year, I was already afforded the opportunity to try this ploy out. In 1987, Dr Tonegawa from Japan was awarded the Prize in Medicine for a discovery concerning the immune system of the body. At the gathering on the 9th, there was a dreadful crowd around him, and it was not eased by the fact that he carried his little son in his arms. The little boy was clearly suffering from a heavy cold which he generously shared with those around him with the help of explosive sneezes. Dr Tonegawa promised to come for a chat in front of the cameras the next evening, to talk about everything from viruses to samurai warriors.

Naturally, his son's virus got a good hold of me, and with my mucous membranes rapidly thickening, I realized that my debut as the Nobel commentator was going to be more interesting than I had counted upon. When the moment came, I had the subject for our conversation ready: given all our knowledge about the immune system of the human body, why can't we deal with the simple, common or garden cold? Dr Tonegawa's answer was an amusing and informative expression of popular science about the body's possibilities and restrictions. Sad to relate, he did not have a remedy, drastic as it was efficacious, for my rapidly worsening cold.

The only opportunity of seizing hold of our interview victims, was after they had left the dinner table and had had their few words with the Royal Couple up on the Prince's Gallery. And if it had been difficult to pinpoint them on the previous evening, it was now seven times worse. The Golden Hall was jam-packed with people; it was very noisy too, and the couples were in continuous, whirling movement. Out on the dance floor were some of our own team who acted as scouts, trying to attract the attention of those with whom we had agreed to have a chat. Sometimes this method met with success, sometimes the laureates became lost in a samba or a Viennese waltz, and we had to use plan 'B' until they recalled our little appoint-

Regal temptation. Every year some curious guests go and sit in the royal chairs after the dinner. A freelance queen with her own courtiers.

ment, waiting there with our cameras and microphones in a little cubby hole right next to the Prince's Gallery.

There was another reason why the route out to us from the Golden Hall could take some time. As you left the Golden Hall, there was a bar which acted as a filter. In 1991, the prizes were awarded for the 90th time and this anniversary was celebrated with due pomp and circumstance. The Physics Prize that year was awarded to the colourful Frenchman Pierre-Gilles de Gennes for his work in the area of liquid crystals. Everything was arranged, Mr de Gennes arrived in excellent spirits at the interview location and I started my introduction while looking into the camera. When I then turned to my right to present the first question, there was nobody there to ask! Out of the corner of my eye, I could see him over by the drinks' table, busy helping himself to a large cognac and lighting what looked like some sort of victory cigar. What should I do? I simply had to resort to French manners and with the help of voice and gestures, called him back over. My insights in the subject of liquid crystals were restricted to those digital watches with their flashing numbers showing the time and date. But all attempts at catching the laureate's elegantly designed watch on camera, were in vain. A Frenchman who has just been awarded the Nobel Prize, and is enjoying a fine cognac and a good cigar is hardly going to keep his hands still. So I changed tactics and asked him to confirm that a French fashion house had made an evening dress, the surface of which was covered with these same liquid crystals. Oh yes, indeed, he said. But there were risks connected with that particular dress, he added, giggling with delight. The crystals were sensitive to changes in temperature, and if the lady who was wearing it should dance or do anything else that might raise the temperature, the dress would change colour. It would start blushing, and that can be embarrassing in some situations, don't you think? Mr de Gennes continued to enjoy his drink and cigar, all

the while speculating as to new areas where his liquid crystals could prove useful. The evening was indeed his.

It was fascinating to see how different these researchers were as people, although they worked in the same area of science and towards the same goals. Several discoveries in physics in recent years have centred around the tiniest building blocks of matter, and the efforts of scientists to prove their existence. The particles are so small, that they cannot be observed through any microscope. Their very existence can only be detected by way of various reactions with other elements, where the results reveal that deep, deep inside there are actually particles smaller than any we have previously known. It has always interested me, how a researcher feels about the fact that at some point scientists must come to the end of the road, and accept that there is nothing smaller to discover. I had the opportunity of asking such questions of a number of the sharpest brains in physics, after a number of Nobel Banquets. The answers differed enormously. Some thought that when we got that far, then that was it, and there was no more to speculate upon. Others were not so sure, and were not prepared to exclude some form of spiritual architect above and beyond what they could see in their laboratories, and measure with their instruments. It was reassuring to hear representatives for the exact sciences come with such approximate answers to these ultimate questions. Ten years earlier, such uncertainty would have been frowned on, and would certainly not have been given publicity.

Being a full-time research scientist at a high level and simultaneously having students to supervise, does not sound like an ideal situation for having a family. However, most of the laureates lived a family life, and indeed several of them pointed out how important it was to mix with non-scientists because otherwise you would run the risk of becoming a recluse or an eccentric. It was also striking, the extent to which research

scientists devoted themselves to very demanding activities in their limited free time. Many extolled the virtues of mountain climbing as the ultimate challenge. Many researchers had, at a ripe old age, gone in for conquering mountain peaks in Germany, Canada and the United States. It seemed not only to be about keeping fit, but was just as much a question of adopting an adequate strategy which would lead to a final result, in this case the peak itself. The same attitude on the mountain as in the laboratory.

It was especially fun when talking with the laureates in the economic sciences, and ask them what they would do with their prize money. Their recipes as to how to invest the money wisely so that it would increase in value, varied considerably from person to person. They did however have one thing in common, regardless of the theories behind their prize, and that was a penchant for investing in real estate. A house, a new sail for the boat, an environmentally friendly car for the wife. But playing stock markets did not seem to be an automatic path to happiness and success, as several of them said, and in reply to my question of what their advice would be if I should win the equivalent sum, the answer which came with uncanny frequency was: invest it carefully.

Many laureates told of their habit of sitting in front of the stereo at home to cleanse and vivify their minds with the help of classical music and opera. In so doing, they could enter new worlds without having to think about measurement or quantification, and it was not impossible that new ideas for further research could also strike them whilst indulging.

Music has of course always been part and parcel of the banquet in the Blue Hall, but one particular occasion remains fixed in my memory. The Russian cellist Mstislav Rostropovich and his wife, the opera singer Galina Visnevskaya were invited one year. Rostropovich was to play something, but also give a speech in memory of his friend Boris Pasternak, who had been awarded the Prize in Literature in 1958. Rostropovich arrived with his cello in the morning to check the acoustics in the Blue Hall. When he saw the tables and everybody busy with place settings, he thought he had been asked to play at a restaurant. I was hovering in the vicinity, hoping to prepare the ground for an interview in the evening. Eventually he was satisfied with where he was to play and the sound, and I made my approach. Mr Rostropovich was faster, and addressed me in English: "Come with me, you help me!" Naturally, but what was I to do? Rostropovich took me down the stairs, under the arches and into a room, converted into a dressing room for the day. There sat his wife, Galina, who looked at me as if I was something the cat had brought in. "You got pen?" Well, luckily I did have a pen of gilded matt steel, a very elegant piece and decidedly suitable for this occasion. Rostropovich took the pen, unfolded a sheet of paper and ordered: "You read in English, I then write in Russian. Must read speech in Russian to my friend Pasternak." And there I stood in the dressing room with two international artistes, one of whom ignored me completely while the other looked sharply at me while sentence after sentence of the speech was transformed from English to Russian. Rostropovich took his time and mumbled in Russian while my pen scraped down word after word. Finally we compared the two versions, sentence by sentence, and everything seemed to be in order. Rostropovich gave me a bear-hug and before I knew it, I was out in the Blue Hall again. I later discovered that my fine pen was missing, but on the other hand: if somebody is going to steal your favourite pen, then only the best is good enough. I hope the ink lasted a long time.

IT IS FINALLY TIME for the moment of truth. This banquet too, sometimes called the banquet of banquets, must come to an end. And even though not everyone will have expe-

In the kitchens, those with the most stamina round off the night with a little snack.
Then the best of all awaits – sleep.

The Nobel Prize Awards 1901–2000

THE NOBEL PRIZE IN PHYSICS

1901
Wilhelm Conrad Röntgen

1902
Hendrik Antoon Lorentz
Pieter Zeeman

1903
Antoine Henri Becquerel
Pierre Curie
Marie Curie

1904
Lord (John William Strutt) Rayleigh

1905
Philipp Eduard Anton von Lenard

1906
Sir Joseph John Thomson

1907
Albert Abraham Michelson

1908
Gabriel Lippmann

1909
Guglielmo Marconi
Carl Ferdinand Braun

1910
Johannes Diderik van der Waals

1911
Wilhelm Wien

1912
Nils Gustaf Dalén

1913
Heike Kamerlingh-Onnes

1914
Max von Laue

1915
Sir William Henry Bragg
William Lawrence Bragg

1916
*The prize money was allocated to
the Special Fund of this prize section.*

1917
Charles Glover Barkla

1918
Max Karl Ernst Ludwig Planck

1919
Johannes Stark

1920
Charles Edouard Guillaume

1921
Albert Einstein

1922
Niels Henrik David Bohr

1923
Robert Andrews Millikan

1924
Karl Manne Georg Siegbahn

1925
James Franck
Gustav Ludwig Hertz

1926
Jean Baptiste Perrin

1927
Arthur Holly Compton
Charles Thomson Rees Wilson

1928
Owen Willans Richardson

1929
Prince Louis-Victor Pierre Raymond
de Broglie

1930
Sir Chandrasekhara Venkata Raman

1931
*The prize money was allocated to
the Special Fund of this prize section.*

1932
Werner Karl Heisenberg

1933
Erwin Schrödinger
Paul Adrien Maurice Dirac

1934
*The prize money was with $1/3$ allocated
to the Main Fund and with $2/3$ to the Special
Fund of this prize section.*

1935
James Chadwick

1936
Victor Franz Hess
Carl David Anderson

1937
Clinton Joseph Davisson
George Paget Thomson

1938
Enrico Fermi

1939
Ernest Orlando Lawrence

1940
*The prize money was with $1/3$ allocated
to the Main Fund and with $2/3$ to the Special
Fund of this prize section.*

1941
*The prize money was with $1/3$ allocated
to the Main Fund and with $2/3$ to the Special
Fund of this prize section.*

1942
*The prize money was with $1/3$ allocated to the
Main Fund and with $2/3$ to the Special Fund of
this prize section.*

1943
Otto Stern

1944
Isidor Isaac Rabi

1945
Wolfgang Pauli

1946
Percy Williams Bridgman

1947
Sir Edward Victor Appleton

1948
Patrick Maynard Stuart Blackett

1949
Hideki Yukawa

1950
Cecil Frank Powell

1951
Sir John Douglas Cockcroft
Ernest Thomas Sinton Walton

1952
Felix Bloch
Edward Mills Purcell

1953
Frits (Frederik) Zernike

1954
Max Born
Walther Bothe

1955
Willis Eugene Lamb
Polykarp Kusch

1956
William Bradford Shockley
John Bardeen
Walter Houser Brattain

1957
Chen Ning Yang
Tsung-Dao Lee

1958
Pavel Alekseyevich Cherenkov
Il'ja Mikhailovich Frank
Igor Yergenyevich Tamm

1959
Emilio Gino Segrè
Owen Chamberlain

1960
Donald Arthur Glaser

1961
Robert Hofstadter
Rudolf Ludwig Mössbauer

1962
Lev Davidovich Landau

1963
Eugene Paul Wigner
Maria Goeppert-Mayer
J. Hans D. Jensen

1964
Charles Hard Townes
Nicolay Gennadiyevich Basov
Aleksandr Mikhailovich Prokhorov

1965
Sin-Itiro Tomonaga
Julian Schwinger
Richard P. Feynman

1966
Alfred Kastler

1967
Hans Albrecht Bethe

1968
Luis Walter Alvarez

1969
Murray Gell-Mann

1970
Hannes Olof Gösta Alfvén
Louis Eugène Félix Néel

1971
Dennis Gabor

1972
John Bardeen
Leon Neil Cooper
John Robert Schrieffer

1973
Leo Esaki
Ivar Giaever
Brian David Josephson

1974
Sir Martin Ryle
Antony Hewish

1975
Aage Niels Bohr
Ben Roy Mottelson
Leo James Rainwater

1976
Burton Richter
Samuel Chao Chung Ting

1977
Philip Warren Anderson
Sir Nevill Francis Mott
John Hasbrouck van Vleck

1978
Pyotr Leonidovich Kapitsa
Arno Allan Penzias
Robert Woodrow Wilson

1979
Sheldon Lee Glashow
Abdus Salam
Steven Weinberg

1980
James Watson Cronin
Val Logsdon Fitch

1981
Nicolaas Bloembergen
Arthur Leonard Schawlow
Kai M. Siegbahn

1982
Kenneth G. Wilson

1983
Subramanyan Chandrasekhar
William Alfred Fowler

1984
Carlo Rubbia
Simon van der Meer

1985
Klaus von Klitzing

1986
Ernst Ruska
Gerd Binnig
Heinrich Rohrer

1987
J. Georg Bednorz
K. Alexander Müller

1988
Leon M. Lederman
Melvin Schwartz
Jack Steinberger

1989
Norman F. Ramsey
Hans G. Dehmelt
Wolfgang Paul

1990
Jerome I. Friedman
Henry W. Kendall
Richard E. Taylor

1991
Pierre-Gilles de Gennes

1992
Georges Charpak

1993
Russell A. Hulse
Joseph H. Taylor Jr.

1994
Bertram N. Brockhouse
Clifford G. Shull

1995
Martin L. Perl
Frederick Reines

1996
David M. Lee
Douglas D. Osheroff
Robert C. Richardson

1997
Steven Chu
Claude Cohen-Tannoudji
William D. Phillips

1998
Robert B. Laughlin
Horst L. Störmer
Daniel C. Tsui

1999
Gerardus 't Hooft
Martinus J.G. Veltman

2000
Zhores I. Alferov
Herbert Kroemer
Jack S. Kilby

THE NOBEL PRIZE IN CHEMISTRY

1901
Jacobus Henricus van 't Hoff

1902
Hermann Emil Fischer

1903
Svante August Arrhenius

1904
Sir William Ramsay

1905
Johann Friedrich Wilhelm Adolf
von Baeyer

1906
Henri Moissan

1907
Eduard Buchner

1908
Ernest Rutherford

1909
Wilhelm Ostwald

1910
Otto Wallach

1911
Marie Curie

1912
Victor Grignard
Paul Sabatier

1913
Alfred Werner

1914
Theodore William Richards

1915
Richard Martin Willstätter

1916
*The prize money was allocated to
the Special Fund of this prize section.*

1917
*The prize money was allocated to
the Special Fund of this prize section.*

1918
Fritz Haber

1919
*The prize money was allocated to
the Special Fund of this prize section.*

1920
Walther Hermann Nernst

1921
Frederick Soddy

1922
Francis William Aston

1923
Fritz Pregl

1924
The prize money was allocated to the
Special Fund of this prize section

1925
Richard Adolf Zsigmondy

1926
The (Theodor) Svedberg

1927
Heinrich Otto Wieland

1928
Adolf Otto Reinhold Windaus

1929
Arthur Harden
Hans Karl August Simon
von Euler-Chelpin

1930
Hans Fischer

1931
Carl Bosch
Friedrich Bergius

1932
Irving Langmuir

1933
*The prize money was with 1/3 allocated
to the Main Fund and with 2/3 to the Special
Fund of this prize section.*

1934
Harold Clayton Urey

1935
Frédéric Joliot
Irène Joliot-Curie

1936
Petrus (Peter) Josephus Wilhelmus Debye

1937
Walter Norman Haworth
Paul Karrer

1938
Richard Kuhn

1939
Adolf Friedrich Johann Butenandt
Leopold Ruzicka

1940
*The prize money was with 1/3 allocated
to the Main Fund and with 2/3 to the Special
Fund of this prize section.*

1941
*The prize money was with 1/3 allocated
to the Main Fund and with 2/3 to the Special
Fund of this prize section.*

1942
*The prize money was with 1/3 allocated
to the Main Fund and with 2/3 to the Special
Fund of this prize section.*

1943
George de Hevesy

1944
Otto Hahn

1945
Artturi Ilmari Virtanen

1946
James Batcheller Sumner
John Howard Northrop
Wendell Meredith Stanley

1947
Sir Robert Robinson

1948
Arne Wilhelm Kaurin Tiselius

1949
William Francis Giauque

1950
Otto, Paul Hermann Diels
Kurt Alder

1951
Edwin Mattison McMillan
Glenn Theodore Seaborg

1952
Archer John Porter Martin
Richard Laurence Millington Synge

1953
Hermann Staudinger

1954
Linus Carl Pauling

1955
Vincent du Vigneaud

1956
Sir Cyril Norman Hinshelwood
Nikolay Nikolaevich Semenov

1957
Lord Alexander R. Todd

1958
Frederick Sanger

1959
Jaroslav Heyrovsky

1960
Willard Frank Libby

1961
Melvin Calvin

1962
Max Ferdinand Perutz
John Cowdery Kendrew

1963
Karl Ziegler
Giulio Natta

1964
Dorothy Crowfoot Hodgkin

1965
Robert Burns Woodward

1966
Robert S. Mulliken

1967
Manfred Eigen
Ronald George Wreyford Norrish
George Porter

1968
Lars Onsager

1969
Derek H. R. Barton
Odd Hassel

1970
Luis F. Leloir

1971
Gerhard Herzberg

1972
Christian B. Anfinsen
Stanford Moore
William H. Stein

1973
Ernst Otto Fischer
Geoffrey Wilkinson

1974
Paul J. Flory

1975
John Warcup Cornforth
Vladimir Prelog

1976
William N. Lipscomb

1977
Ilya Prigogine

1978
Peter D. Mitchell

1979
Herbert C. Brown
Georg Wittig

1980
Paul Berg
Walter Gilbert
Frederick Sanger

1981
Kenichi Fukui
Roald Hoffmann

1982
Aaron Klug

1983
Henry Taube

1984
Robert Bruce Merrifield

1985
Herbert A. Hauptman
Jerome Karle

1986
Dudley R. Herschbach
Yuan T. Lee
John C. Polanyi

1987
Donald J. Cram
Jean-Marie Lehn
Charles J. Pedersen

1988
Johann Deisenhofer
Robert Huber
Hartmut Michel

1989
Sidney Altman
Thomas R. Cech

1990
Elias James Corey

1991
Richard R. Ernst

1992
Rudolph A. Marcus

1993
Kary B. Mullis
Michael Smith

1994
George A. Olah

1995
Paul J. Crutzen
Mario J. Molina
F. Sherwood Rowland

1996
Robert F. Curl Jr.
Sir Harold W. Kroto
Richard E. Smalley

1997
Paul D. Boyer
John E. Walker
Jens C. Skou

1998
Walter Kohn
John A. Pople

1999
Ahmed H. Zewail

2000
Alan J. Heeger
Alan G. MacDiarmid
Hideki Shirakawa

THE NOBEL PRIZE IN PHYSIOLOGY OR MEDICINE

1901
Emil Adolf von Behring

1902
Ronald Ross

1903
Niels Ryberg Finsen

1904
Ivan Petrovich Pavlov

1905
Robert Koch

1906
Camillo Golgi
Santiago Ramón Y Cajal

1907
Charles Louis Alphonse Laveran

1908
Ilya Ilyich Mechnikov
Paul Ehrlich

1909
Emil Theodor Kocher

1910
Albrecht Kossel

1911
Allvar Gullstrand

1912
Alexis Carrel

1913
Charles Robert Richet

1914
Robert Bárány

1915
The prize money was allocated to the Special Fund of this prize section.

1916
The prize money was allocated to the Special Fund of this prize section.

1917
The prize money was allocated to the Special Fund of this prize section.

1918
The prize money was allocated to the Special Fund of this prize section.

1919
Jules Bordet

1920
Schack August Steenberg Krogh

1921
The prize money was allocated to the Special Fund of this prize section.

1922
Archibald Vivian Hill
Otto Fritz Meyerhof

1923
Frederick Grant Banting
John James Richard Macleod

1924
Willem Einthoven

1925
The prize money was allocated to the Special Fund of this prize section.

1926
Johannes Andreas Grib Fibiger

1927
Julius Wagner-Jauregg

1928
Charles Jules Henri Nicolle

1929
Christiaan Eijkman
Sir Frederick Gowland Hopkins

1930
Karl Landsteiner

1931
Otto Heinrich Warburg

1932
Sir Charles Scott Sherrington
Edgar Douglas Adrian

1933
Thomas Hunt Morgan

1934
George Hoyt Whipple
George Richards Minot
William Parry Murphy

1935
Hans Spemann

1936
Sir Henry Hallett Dale
Otto Loewi

1937
Albert von Szent-Györgyi Nagyrapolt

1938
Corneille Jean François Heymans

1939
Gerhard Domagk

1940
*The prize money was with 1/3 allocated
to the Main Fund and with 2/3 to the Special
Fund of this prize section.*

1941
*The prize money was with 1/3 allocated
to the Main Fund and with 2/3 to the Special
Fund of this prize section.*

1942
*The prize money was with 1/3 allocated
to the Main Fund and with 2/3 to the Special
Fund of this prize section.*

1943
Henrik Carl Peter Dam
Edward Adelbert Doisy

1944
Joseph Erlanger
Herbert Spencer Gasser

1945
Sir Alexander Fleming
Ernst Boris Chain
Sir Howard Walter Florey

1946
Hermann Joseph Muller

1947
Carl Ferdinand Cori
Gerty Theresa, née Radnitz Cori
Bernardo Alberto Houssay

1948
Paul Hermann Müller

1949
Walter Rudolf Hess
Antonio Caetano De Abreu Freire Egas
Moniz

1950
Edward Calvin Kendall
Tadeus Reichstein
Philip Showalter Hench

1951
Max Theiler

1952
Selman Abraham Waksman

1953
Hans Adolf Krebs
Fritz Albert Lipmann

1954
John Franklin Enders
Thomas Huckle Weller
Frederick Chapman Robbins

1955
Axel Hugo Theodor Theorell

1956
André Frédéric Cournand
Werner Forssmann
Dickinson W. Richards

1957
Daniel Bovet

1958
George Wells Beadle
Edward Lawrie Tatum
Joshua Lederberg

1959
Severo Ochoa
Arthur Kornberg

1960
Sir Frank Macfarlane Burnet
Peter Brian Medawar

1961
Georg von Békésy

1962
Francis Harry Compton Crick
James Dewey Watson
Maurice Hugh Frederick Wilkins

1963
Sir John Carew Eccles
Alan Lloyd Hodgkin
Andrew Fielding Huxley

1964
Konrad Bloch
Feodor Lynen

1965
François Jacob
André Lwoff
Jacques Monod

1966
Peyton Rous
Charles Brenton Huggins

1967
Ragnar Granit
Haldan Keffer Hartline
George Wald

1968
Robert W. Holley
Har Gobind Khorana
Marshall W. Nirenberg

1969
Max Delbrück
Alfred D. Hershey
Salvador E. Luria

1970
Sir Bernard Katz
Ulf von Euler
Julius Axelrod

1971
Earl W. Sutherland, Jr.

1972
Gerald M. Edelman
Rodney R. Porter

1973
Karl von Frisch
Konrad Lorenz
Nikolaas Tinbergen

1974
Albert Claude
Christian de Duve
George E. Palade

1975
David Baltimore
Renato Dulbecco
Howard Martin Temin

1976
Baruch S. Blumberg
D. Carleton Gajdusek

1977
Roger Guillemin
Andrew V. Schally
Rosalyn Yalow

1978
Werner Arber
Daniel Nathans
Hamilton O. Smith

1979
Allan M. Cormack
Godfrey N. Hounsfield

1980
Baruj Benacerraf
Jean Dausset
George D. Snell

1981
Roger W. Sperry
David H. Hubel
Torsten N. Wiesel

1982
Sune K. Bergström
Bengt I. Samuelsson
John R. Vane

1983
Barbara McClintock

1984
Niels K. Jerne
Georges J.F. Köhler
César Milstein

1985
Michael S. Brown
Joseph L. Goldstein

1986
Stanley Cohen
Rita Levi-Montalcini

1987
Susumu Tonegawa

1988
Sir James W. Black
Gertrude B. Elion
George H. Hitchings

1989
J. Michael Bishop
Harold E. Varmus

1990
Joseph E. Murray
E. Donnall Thomas

1991
Erwin Neher
Bert Sakmann

1992
Edmond H. Fischer
Edwin G. Krebs

1993
Richard J. Roberts
Phillip A. Sharp

1994
Alfred G. Gilman
Martin Rodbell

1995
Edward B. Lewis
Christiane Nüsslein-Volhard
Eric F. Wieschaus

1996
Peter C. Doherty
Rolf M. Zinkernagel

1997
Stanley B. Prusiner

1998
Robert F. Furchgott
Louis J. Ignarro
Ferid Murad

1999
Günter Blobel

2000
Arvid Carlsson
Paul Greengard
Eric Kandel

THE NOBEL PRIZE IN LITERATURE

1901
Sully Prudhomme (pen-name of
René François Armand Prudhomme)

1902
Christian Matthias Theodor Mommsen

1903
Bjørnstjerne Martinus Bjørnson

1904
Frédéric Mistral
José Echegaray Y Eizaguirre

1905
Henryk Sienkiewicz

1906
Giosuè Carducci

1907
Rudyard Kipling

1908
Rudolf Christoph Eucken

1909
Selma Ottilia Lovisa Lagerlöf

1910
Paul Johann Ludwig Heyse

1911
Count Maurice (Mooris) Polidore Marie
Bernhard Maeterlinck

1912
Gerhart Johann Robert Hauptmann

1913
Rabindranath Tagore

1914
*The prize money was allocated to
the Special Fund of this prize section.*

1915
Romain Rolland

1916
Carl Gustaf Verner von Heidenstam

1917
Karl Adolph Gjellerup
Henrik Pontoppidan

1918
*The prize money was allocated to
the Special Fund of this prize section.*

1919
Carl Friedrich Georg Spitteler

1920
Knut Pedersen Hamsun

1921
Anatole France (pen-name of
Jacques Anatole Thibault)

1922
Jacinto Benavente

1923
William Butler Yeats

1924
Wladyslaw Stanislaw Reymont
(pen-name of Reyment)

1925
George Bernard Shaw

1926
Grazia Deledda (pen-name of
Grazia Madesani née Deledda)

1927
Henri Bergson

1928
Sigrid Undset

1929
Thomas Mann

1930
Sinclair Lewis

1931
Erik Axel Karlfeldt

1932
John Galsworthy

1933
Ivan Alekseyevich Bunin

1934
Luigi Pirandello

1935
*The prize money was with 1/3 allocated
to the Main Fund and with 2/3 to the Special
Fund of this prize section.*

1936
Eugene Gladstone O'Neill

1937
Roger Martin du Gard

1938
Pearl Buck (pen-name of
Pearl Walsh née Sydenstricker)

1939
Frans Eemil Sillanpää

1940
*The prize money was with 1/3 allocated
to the Main Fund and with 2/3 to the Special
Fund of this prize section.*

1941
*The prize money was with 1/3 allocated
to the Main Fund and with 2/3 to the Special
Fund of this prize section.*

1942
*The prize money was with 1/3 allocated
to the Main Fund and with 2/3 to the Special
Fund of this prize section.*

1943
*The prize money was with 1/3 allocated
to the Main Fund and with 2/3 to the Special
Fund of this prize section.*

1944
Johannes Vilhelm Jensen

1945
Gabriela Mistral (pen-name of
Lucila Godoy Y Alcayaga)

1946
Hermann Hesse

1947
André Paul Guillaume Gide

1948
Thomas Stearns Eliot

1949
William Faulkner

1950
Earl (Bertrand Arthur William) Russell

1951
Pär Fabian Lagerkvist

1952
François Mauriac

1953
Sir Winston Leonard Spencer Churchill

1954
Ernest Miller Hemingway

1955
Halldór Kiljan Laxness

1956
Juan Ramón Jiménez

1957
Albert Camus

1958
Boris Leonidovich Pasternak

1959
Salvatore Quasimodo

1960
Saint-John Perse (pen-name of
Alexis Léger)

1961
Ivo Andric

1962
John Steinbeck

1963
Giorgos Seferis (pen-name of
Giorgos Seferiadis)

1964
Jean-Paul Sartre

1965
Michail Aleksandrovich Sholokhov

1966
Shmuel Yosef Agnon
Nelly Sachs

1967
Miguel Angel Asturias

1968
Yasunari Kawabata

1969
Samuel Beckett

1970
Aleksandr Isaevich Solzhenitsyn

1971
Pablo Neruda (pen-name of
Neftali Ricardo Reyes Basoalto)

1972
Heinrich Böll

1973
Patrick White

1974
Eyvind Johnson
Harry Martinson

1975
Eugenio Montale

1976
Saul Bellow

1977
Vicente Aleixandre

1978
Isaac Bashevis Singer

1979
Odysseus Elytis (pen-name of
Odysseus Alepoudhelis)

1980
Czeslaw Milosz

1981
Elias Canetti

1982
Gabriel García Márquez

1983
William Golding

1984
Jaroslav Seifert

1985
Claude Simon

1986
Wole Soyinka

1987
Joseph Brodsky

1988
Naguib Mahfouz

1989
Camilo José Cela

1990
Octavio Paz

1991
Nadine Gordimer

1992
Derek Walcott

1993
Toni Morrison

1994
Kenzaburo Oe

1995
Seamus Heaney

1996
Wislawa Szymborska

1997
Dario Fo

1998
José Saramago

1999
Günter Grass

2000
Gao Xingjian

TEH NOBEL PEACE PRIZE

1901
Jean Henri Dunant
Frédéric Passy

1902
Élie Ducommun
Charles Albert Gobat

1903
William Randal Cremer

1904
Institut de droit international
(Institute of International Law)

1905
Baroness Bertha Sophie Felicita,
née Countess Kinsky von Chinic
und Tettau von Suttner

1906
Theodore Roosevelt

1907
Ernesto Teodoro Moneta
Louis Renault

1908
Klas Pontus Arnoldson
Fredrik Bajer

1909
Auguste Marie François Beernaert
Paul Henri Benjamin Balluet, Baron De
Constant De Rebecque d'Estournelle De
Constant

1910
Bureau international permanent de la Paix
(Permanent International Peace Bureau)

1911
Tobias Michael Carel Asser
Alfred Hermann Fried

1912
Elihu Root

1913
Henri La Fontaine

1914
*The prize money was allocated to
the Special Fund of this prize section.*

1915
The prize money was allocated to the Special Fund of this prize section.

1916
The prize money was allocated to the Special Fund of this prize section.

1917
Comité international de la Croix Rouge (International Committee of the Red Cross

1918
The prize money was allocated to the Special Fund of this prize section.

1919
Thomas Woodrow Wilson

1920
Léon Victor Auguste Bourgeois

1921
Karl Hjalmar Branting
Christian Lous Lange

1922
Fridtjof Nansen

1923
The prize money was allocated to the Special Fund of this prize section.

1924
The prize money was allocated to the Special Fund of this prize section.

1925
Sir Austen Chamberlain
Charles Gates Dawes

1926
Aristide Briand
Gustav Stresemann

1927
Ferdinand Buisson
Ludwig Quidde

1928
The prize money was allocated to the Special Fund of this prize section.

1929
Frank Billings Kellogg

1930
Lars Olof Nathan (Jonathan) Söderblom

1931
Jane Addams
Nicholas Murray Butler

1932
The prize money was allocated to the Special Fund of this prize section.

1933
Sir Norman Angell (Ralph Lane)

1934
Arthur Henderson

1935
Carl von Ossietzky

1936
Carlos Saavedra Lamas

1937
Viscount, (Lord Edgar Algernon Robert Gascoyne Cecil) Cecil Of Chelwood

1938
Office international Nansen pour les Réfugiés (Nansen International Office for Refugees)

1939
The prize money was with 1/3 allocated to the Main Fund and with 2/3 to the Special Fund of this prize section.

1940
The prize money was with 1/3 allocated to the Main Fund and with 2/3 to the Special Fund of this prize section.

1941
The prize money was with 1/3 allocated to the Main Fund and with 2/3 to the Special Fund of this prize section.

1942
The prize money was with 1/3 allocated to the Main Fund and with 2/3 to the Special Fund of this prize section.

1943
The prize money was with 1/3 allocated to the Main Fund and with 2/3 to the Special Fund of this prize section.

1944
Comité international de la Croix Rouge (International Committee of the Red Cross

1945
Cordell Hull

1946
Emily Greene Balch
John Raleigh Mott

1947
Friends Service Council (The Quakers)
American Friends Service Committee (The Quakers)

1948
The prize money was with 1/3 allocated to the Main Fund and with 2/3 to the Special Fund of this prize section.

1949
Lord (John) Boyd Orr Of Brechin

1950
Ralph Bunche

1951
Léon Jouhaux

1952
Albert Schweitzer

1953
George Catlett Marshall

1954
Office of the United Nations High Commissioner for Refugees

1955
The prize money was with 1/3 allocated to the Main Fund and with 2/3 to the Special Fund of this prize section.

1956
The prize money was with 1/3 allocated to the Main Fund and with 2/3 to the Special Fund of this prize section.

1957
Lester Bowles Pearson

1958
Georges Pire

1959
Philip J. Noel-Baker

1960
Albert John Lutuli

1961
Dag Hjalmar Agne Carl Hammarskjöld

1962
Linus Carl Pauling

1963
Comité international de la Croix Rouge (International Committee of the Red Cross
Ligue des Sociétés de la Croix-Rouge (League of Red Cross Societies)

1964
Martin Luther King Jr.

1965
United Nations Children's Fund (UNICEF)

1966
The prize money was with 1/3 allocated to the Main Fund and with 2/3 to the Special Fund of this prize section.

1967
The prize money was with 1/3 allocated to the Main Fund and with 2/3 to the Special Fund of this prize section.

1968
René Cassin

1969
International Labour Organization (I.L.O.)

1970
Norman Borlaug

1971
Willy Brandt

1972
The prize money for 1972 was allocated to the Main Fund.

1973
Henry, A. Kissinger
Le Duc Tho

1974
Seán MacBride
Eisaku Sato

1975
Andrei Dmitrievich Sakharov

1976
Betty Williams
Mairead Corrigan

1977
Amnesty International

1978
Mohamed Anwar el Sadat
Menachem Begin

1979
Mother Teresa

1980
Adolfo Perez Esquivel

1981
Office of the United Nations High
Commissioner for Refugees

1982
Alva Myrdal
Alfonso García Robles

1983
Lech Walesa

1984
Desmond Mpilo Tutu

1985
International Physicians for the
Prevention of Nuclear War Inc.

1986
Elie Wiesel

1987
Oscar Arias Sanchez

1988
United Nations Peace-keeping Forces

1989
Dalai Lama (Tenzin Gyatso 14Th)

1990
Mikhail Sergeyevich Gorbachev

1991
Aung San Suu Kyi

1992
Rigoberta Menchu Tum

1993
Nelson Mandela
Frederik Willem de Klerk

1994
Yasser Arafat
Shimon Peres
Yitzhak Rabin

1995
Joseph Rotblat
Pugwash Conferences on Science
and World Affairs

1996
Carlos Filipe Ximenes Belo
José Ramos-Horta

1997
International Campaign to Ban
Landmines (Icbl)
Jody Williams

1998
John Hume
David Trimble

1999
Médecins Sans Frontières

2000
Kim Dae Jung

THE BANK OF SWEDEN PRIZE IN ECONOMIC SCIENCES IN MEMORY OF ALFRED NOBEL

1969
Ragnar Frisch
Jan Tinbergen

1970
Paul A Samuelson

1971
Simon Kuznets

1972
John R. Hicks
Kenneth J. Arrow

1973
Wassily Leontief

1974
Gunnar Myrdal
Friedrich August von Hayek

1975
Leonid Vitaliyevich Kantorovich
Tjalling C. Koopmans

1976
Milton Friedman

1977
Bertil Ohlin
James E. Meade

1978
Herbert A. Simon

1979
Theodore W. Schultz
Arthur Lewis

1980
Lawrence R. Klein

1981
James Tobin

1982
George J. Stigler

1983
Gerard Debreu

1984
Richard Stone

1985
Franco Modigliani

1986
James M. Buchanan Jr.

1987
Robert M. Solow

1988
Maurice Allais

1989
Trygve Haavelmo

1990
Harry M. Markowitz
Merton H. Miller
William F. Sharpe

1991
Ronald H. Coase

1992
Gary S. Becker

1993
Robert W. Fogel
Douglass C. North

1994
John C. Harsanyi
John F. Nash Jr.
Reinhard Selten

1995
Robert E. Lucas Jr.

1996
James A. Mirrlees
William Vickrey

1997
Robert C. Merton
Myron S. Scholes

1998
Amartya Sen

1999
Robert A. Mundell

2000
James J. Heckman
Daniel L. McFadden

This book has been published with the support of:

Nordea   Skandia   Volvo

AstraZeneca, D. Carnegie, Stadshuskällaren,
Stockholms Näringslivskontor and Wallenius Wilhelmsen Lines

Thanks to…

Lars Axelsson, publisher of this book, who tragically died in the final stages of this project.
I would like to express my gratitude for having been able to work with Lars,
who was very inspiring in both a professional and a personal sense.

*

I wish to particularly thank *Nils Degerman* of Prisma, who, together with *Lars Axelsson*
had faith in my idea when I came to them with a carton of photographs long ago.

Sven Odqvist, of Active Sponsoring, for creating the economic basis
necessary for the project.

Carl Åkesson for his fine design work and sensitive treatment of the pictures,
and for the way he – together with *Nils Degerman* – has made me discover new sides
in my pictures and my photography.

Niklas Lindblad for contributing with his text which gives a unique insight into
the Nobel festivities.

Scanpix and *Anders Holmström* for allowing me to work on this project while employed
as a photographer, and for supporting me even after I had ceased working for them.

Inger Widell and *Kurt Rickardsson* at Mörkrummet for their work with all the difficult negatives.

Fälth & Hässler, Sweden.

Fujifilm Sverige AB.

And finally to restaurateur *Lars-Göran Andersson* at the City Hall Restaurant
and his staff, for letting me in and being so friendly and helpful.

/Pawel Flato